A
Railway Family
in
India

The Signals Say "Go" (outside Guntakal)

A Railway Family in India

Five Generations of the Stevenages

by

Patrick Hugh Stevenage

BACSA

PUTNEY, LONDON
2001

Published by the British Association
for Cemeteries in South Asia (BACSA)

Secretary: Theon Wilkinson MBE
76½ Chartfield Avenue
London SW15 6HQ

The British Association for Cemeteries in South Asia was formed in 1976 to
preserve, convert and record old European cemeteries.
All proceeds from the sale of this book go towards this charity
(Registered No 273422)

ISBN 0 907799 77 9

British Libraries Cataloguing-in-Publication Data
A catalogue record for this book is available from the British Library

Typeset by Professional Presentation, 3 Prairie Road, Addlestone, Surrey

Printed by The Chameleon Press Ltd,5-25 Burr Road, Wandsworth SW18 4SG

Contents

Foreword

A Railway Family In India is the thirty-first in our series of books about Europeans in South Asia, written by BACSA members, published by BACSA with a wider public in mind.

This book covers five generations of one particular family whose adventurous forebear left the shores of England in 1778 at the age of 19 as a private in the East India Company's Madras European Regiment and founded a family in India.

The author, Patrick Stevenage, a direct descendant, father to son for five generations, emigrated to England in 1951 - nearly two centuries later - and in his leisure moments completed this remarkable family saga.

As one reads of the Stevenages from their humble beginnings in India as one of the 'twilight communities of Anglo-Indians', through successive generations in Madras, Bangalore, Cochin, Bellary and so on, one gets a vivid picture of their life, the education and career opportunities open to them and of their recreations.

The author's meticulously researched account of his family is matched by reminiscences and details of his career in the Madras & Southern Mahratta railway in India, and a senior management position within British Rail in England, monitoring the Investment Budget of the Railways Board, some four hundred million pounds per annum.

The Indian railways had an unique place in the social mix within towns and cities where there was a significant European population. They were largely run by 'Anglo-Indians', variously described at different times as 'Eurasians', 'Indo-Britains', 'Country-born', 'Domiciled' etc, constituting a virtually closed railway community with their own schools, hospitals, cemeteries, clubs, sports and entertainments.

Patrick Stevenage needs no introduction, as he has been a staunch supporter of BACSA for over twenty years and we are grateful to him for allowing us to produce this intimate account of his family which will appeal to all those who enjoy reading about the different aspects of India, and in particular to the railway enthusiast and genealogist.

In memory

of my beloved mother,

Helena Augusta Stevenage.

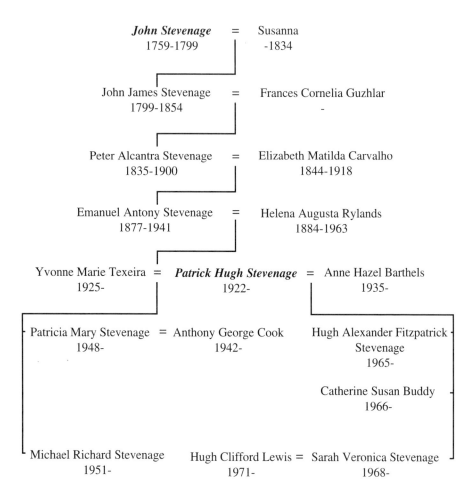

John Stevenage = Susanna
1759-1799 -1834

John James Stevenage = Frances Cornelia Guzhlar
1799-1854 -

Peter Alcantra Stevenage = Elizabeth Matilda Carvalho
1835-1900 1844-1918

Emanuel Antony Stevenage = Helena Augusta Rylands
1877-1941 1884-1963

Yvonne Marie Texeira = *Patrick Hugh Stevenage* = Anne Hazel Barthels
1925- 1922- 1935-

Patricia Mary Stevenage = Anthony George Cook   Hugh Alexander Fitzpatrick
1948- 1942- Stevenage
1965-

Catherine Susan Buddy
1966-

Michael Richard Stevenage   Hugh Clifford Lewis = Sarah Veronica Stevenage
1951- 1971- 1968-

Part I - My Ancestors

The Voyage To India

A decisive step in the history of the Stevenage family was taken in 1778, when John Stevenage decided to seek his fortune abroad.

All England had thrilled to the military exploits of Robert Clive, clerk turned soldier extraordinary. The huge fortunes accumulated with seeming ease by the 'Nabobs' dazzled and excited the envy of the nation. Eyes turned towards 'The Golden East' and the Honourable East India Company firmly held the key of the door. For British subjects, entrance into India was possible only with their permission and normally through the cadres of their civil or military services.

John enlisted as a private in the Company's Madras European Regiment and the records preserved at the Oriental & India Office Collections, London, show that he was then aged 19 years and stood 5 foot 3 inches in height, the minimum requirements at that time. He described himself as a native of Surrey and gave his former occupation as 'glazier'. He did not name his parish.

John entered the service of the Company on 25th March 1778, and, at Gravesend on 8th April, he was mustered aboard the Indiaman *Stafford* bound for Madras on the Coromandel coast. A fleet was gathering off the Downs in preparation for the long voyage to India. It was the usual practice for ships to sail in convoy for protection against pirates and the enemies of the Crown. There was also the advantage of mutual aid in the face of natural hazards.

On 20th April, John was one of a squad of men transferred from the *Stafford* to the *Colebrooke*, another ship of the fleet. The reason for the move emerged on 7th May when Sir Eyre Coote, the new Commander-in-Chief in India, his wife, secretary, ADC, physician and nine European servants all embarked on the *Stafford*. At last the great sails were unfurled and the adventure commenced.

The *Colebrooke* was a well founded ship of 723 tons and the log kept by Captain Arthur Morris was fairly routine until:

24th August 1778 – Ship is in False Bay

11.30 am – Struck a rock which was unseen from the masthead – got her free from the rock but she fouled again.

The *Gatton* not being above two ships' lengths astern – advised her and she escaped the danger. The *Asia* and the *Royal Admiral* being astern we fired a

1

gun and hoisted the ensign union downwards. The *Patter* kept her wind and passed a mile to windward. We manned the pumps as we had now shipped 15 inches of water. Hailed the *Gatton* for assistance. Boats from the *Asia* and the *Gatton* came alongside and put some hands aboard. The ship came off the rock and we made sail so as to get as far up the bay as possible. At the inner point of Cape Bona at W.S.W. at about 4 miles. The Bellows bore 4 to 5 miles. The bearings must not be looked upon as being exact as no telling how the shock of the impact affected the compass. In this dreadful situation a conference of the Officers was held by Capt. Morris. Decided to make for a sandy bay and ground the ship.

4 pm – Went aground in sandy bay and the ship settled hard. Boats from the *Asia*, the *Gatton* and the *Royal Admiral* came alongside and took on passengers and tried to effect a landing on sandy beach. Put Honourable Company's packet into the pinnace with about 20 hands and sent her towards the shore but unfortunately she overturned and several hands lost their lives. Hoisted the longboat at sunset and sent her ahead of the ship to attach a grapnel. None of the small boats being able to land, put their people into the longboat.

10 pm – A boat hailed us and told us that the longboat had drove ashore with all the people. It was a very dark and dismal night especially for the people who longed ardently for daylight.

25th August 1778, *7 am* – A boat from the *Asia* came alongside and took off Captain Morris, the fourth mate, the surgeon, the purser, and as many more as he could hold. We had the satisfaction of seeing our longboat pulling up alongshore to the south. The *Gatton's* cutter came alongside. Sent women passengers and some others to the longboat. Launched the raft overside and sent about 12 people on it but unfortunately it overset in the surf and 5 or 6 people were lost. The *Royal Admiral's* boat not choosing to come alongside hailed her to go to the assistance of the longboat which she did not comply with. The third mate of the *Royal Admiral* floated a line ashore which was made fast and a raft was hauled to and from the shore and several successful trips were made sending 9 or 10 people at a time.

10 am – We have got almost everybody out of the ship with the loss of 2 or 3 that were washed off the raft.

10.30 am – The officers got into the *Gatton's* boat and went back to the *Gatton*. Learned that the *Asia's* cutter had arrived back safe. Could learn nothing of the longboat. Made landing from the cutter and marched overland and came upon some of our people. They came down in large parties and we marched to the landing place. Could not take them on board but told them to wait at the landing place until morning when boats would be sent for them. They informed us of the loss of the gunner's mate and about 12 more people. This evening received the agreeable news that the longboat having drove ashore at the bottom of False Bay, everybody was safe. Visited the wreck and hailed the people ashore and told them to proceed overland.

26th August 1778 – Went inshore on the boats. Could not see any of our people. Presumed that they had proceeded by land.

After a short rest at Cape Town the survivors of the *Colebrooke* were crowded onto the remainder of the fleet and eventually, at the end of December, the convoy stood off the sandy beach of Fort St George, Madras. Almost at once the *masula* boats crowded around and began to ferry people ashore, plunging through the surf until they were close enough to wade, or be carried the last few yards to the wide expanse of sand before the fort gate.

On the Long Roll of the Company's Establishment at Madras, the name of John Stevenage appears for the first time on 2nd January 1779. The record shows that he had landed from the *Stafford*.

Extract from 'CHOWKIDAR' – Volume 7 No.2, Page 28: Autumn 1994

BACSA member R.R.Langham -Carter, writing from South Africa, reminds us that shipwrecks on the Eastern run were common in the old days, and that many a passenger found a watery grave instead of lying in a cemetery in South Asia. The *Dalhousie* captained by John Butterworth, sank with all hands in the English Channel, in 1853, just a few days out. Another such ship was the *Colebrooke*, an East Indiaman of 739 tons, named for Sir Edward Colebrooke, a Director of the East India Company. Captained by Arthur Morris, she set out from Gravesend on 30th January 1778, bound for Bombay and China, via Madeira with a cargo of lead, copper, cloth, gunpowder and small arms. Also carried were many small items of private trade, like scissors and snuff. At Madeira the *Colebrooke* took on 43 pipes of wine, but on reaching the Cape she was wrecked on the eastern shore of False Bay on 24th August 1778. The bay where she sank is now known as Koeelbaai – an adaptation of her name. Luckily all the passengers and all but three of the crew were saved.

For more than two hundred years the wreck lay undisturbed. It was discovered accidentally by an exploration salvage group in 1984, who found the *Colebrooke* partially covered by three metres of sand. Although this made salvage difficult, it had preserved the ship's contents from decay, and lead and copper ingots, together with musket parts, snuff and scissors were salvaged. The most intriguing items were intact bottles of Madeira, which unfortunately proved to be undrinkable when opened. A new expedition is being mounted this year which should bring further items to light and a better understanding of ship construction during the 18th century.

THE EUROPEAN MAGAZINE, December 1783: FORT ST.GEORGE, MADRAS

When the European nations first began to settle along the western coast of the Bay of Bengal, the English East India Company early formed a settlement at Chilipatam or Madras, which was well situated for the trade there carried on, being nearly the central part of the Coast of Coromandel, and commanding a great part of the trade of the Carnatic. This place is still their principal Settlement on that Coast, and is situated in about 15 degrees North Latitude, and about 80 degrees of Longitude East from London. Being seated within the tropics it experiences all the disadvantages arising from heat which is usual in those latitudes; and, were it not for the sea breezes that daily cool the air, would not be habitable by European constitutions.

The Settlement consists of two towns; that called the White Town is a regular fortification, and is about 400 paces long, and about 150 broad, divided into regular streets, the houses being built with brick, the rooms lofty, and the roofs flat. The Town is a Corporation, and has a Mayor, Aldermen, and other proper Officers; with two churches, one for the Protestants, the other, for the Roman Catholics; also a hospital, a town-hall, and a prison for debtors. The Black Town, which consists chiefly of thatched cottages, is inhabited by Gentoos, Mahomedans, and Portuguese and Armenian Christians, and each religion has its temples and churches.

The whole number of inhabitants in the colony, including the towns and villages in the vicinity of Fort St. George, is computed at about 80,000, who are all dependent upon the Governor and his Council, in whom is lodged all the military power, and who are also the last resort in Civil Cases. In time of war this Settlement may experience the greatest distress, should the enemy possess a superiority at sea, its inhabitants depending for their subsistence upon that element, as their rice is brought from Ganjam and Orixa, their wheat from Surat and Bengal, and their firing from the island of Diu. It not only fronts the sea, but has a salt water river running at its back, whereby the fresh water springs are prevented coming near the town, so that there is no good water within a mile of it.

Notwithstanding these disadvantages its situation for trade will always make it a place of importance, as the diamond mines are but a week's journey from it, consequently they are in tolerable plenty, though they have not produced any of a large size for some time past. The inland trade of the colony is chiefly managed by the Armenians and Gentoos, who largely supply the Company servants with those articles which constitute the export trade, being besides diamonds, callicoes, chintz, muslin and other articles of the like nature.

The number of European inhabitants, including the military, is generally computed at 500 men.

The Wars With Mysore

The Long Roll at Fort St George, Madras, annually recorded the name of John Stevenage from 1779 to 1797. His place of origin, the ship from which he landed and the date of his arrival are repeated with each entry. No additional information is available – no heroic deeds, medals or wounds; no punishments or rewards; no transfers or promotions. Such details could be garnered from various sources only for officers. A blanket of anonymity was spread over the 'Other Ranks', except for the 'hero' and the 'villain'. Presumably John was neither. But if he was largely unrecorded, the Madras in which he found himself was bubbling with adventure and excitement and the Madras European Regiment was in the thick of every action.

The Company's European troops were recruited mainly in Britain and uniformed, armed and disciplined after the fashion of the Royal Army. In Madras their numbers had grown from about 100 in 1645 to four battalions totalling nearly 3,000 officers and men in 1770. The proud colours of the Madras Europeans bore the royal tiger and its battle honours boasted 'Arcot' and 'Plassey'. Each battalion had field guns attached to it, served by men of the battalion. When necessary they also mounted a troop of dragoons and provided their own sappers and engineers.

The French had been forced to surrender Pondicherry, their principal Indian settlement in October 1778 and by March 1779, Mahé had also fallen. Thus the French power bases in south India had been knocked out, at least temporarily. Some of John's earliest memories of India were probably of the arrival of French officers and men captured at these places and brought, with their families, to Madras in April and May 1779. A later batch of French prisoners captured in the continuing saga of Anglo-French wars in south India included a certain Sergeant Bernadotte who was repatriated to France and is better known to history as one of Napoleon's dashing marshals and later as Sweden's king.

But peace was short lived. Hyder Ali, the ruler of Mysore, was ready to resume his interrupted struggle against the British. In 1780 his horsemen swept down on Madras, devastating its suburbs, killing, looting and burning. The natives fled to the fort for protection, the garden houses of the Madras officials went up in flames and from St Thomas' Mount, smoke could be seen rising in every direction. The British had been caught unprepared but reacted to stem the enemy advance. Sir Hector Munro took the field with all available troops, but in September, Colonel Baillie and a small force were almost literally cut to pieces by the Mysore army at Conjeeveram. Sir Hector retreated hastily losing most of his baggage in the process. Fortunately, John could not have been in Baillie's force, of which only a very few broken men finally emerged from the dungeons of Mysore.

Warren Hastings, the Governor General, dismissed the Governor of Madras and hurriedly dispatched Sir Eyre Coote from Calcutta with men, money and express orders to vindicate the rights and honour of British arms. Coote reached Madras on 5th November and with characteristic energy pushed forward the task of refitting and reorganising the army. By January 1781 he was ready to face Hyder Ali but it was not until July that major battle was joined at Porto Novo and this time a costly defeat was inflicted on Mysore. The war was far from over and bitter fighting continued with mounting losses on both sides. 'Sholingur' was added to the battle honour of the Madras Europeans; the French returned to the arena as the allies of Mysore; on many battlefields and in numerous hard fought engagements the honour of British arms was amply vindicated.

When Hyder Ali died suddenly in December 1782, decisive action could have been taken to end the war but Sir Eyre Coote was by then a sick man and while the British dithered, the moment passed. Hyder's son, Tippoo Sultan, secured his father's throne for himself and soon proved that he was an even more formidable opponent than ever his father had been. The war dragged on into 1784 and ended in a patched-up peace which nobody expected would last very long.

Surprisingly, the uneasy peace endured until December 1789 when Tippoo attacked the 'Travancore Lines'. The Madras Army was again called into action and this time they were better prepared. Under General Medows and Lord Cornwallis they advanced, carrying the war deep into Mysore territory. After much marching, manoeuvering and bitter fighting, Bangalore was occupied in March 1791. In October the strong fortress of Nundydroog was stormed and another name was added to the battle honours of the Madras Europeans. The tide was flowing strongly against Tippoo and when the capture of his capital, Seringapatam, seemed imminent in 1792 he sued for peace and offered royal hostages. Yet another peace treaty was signed with Mysore.

The next year Britain and France were again at war and a column from Madras once more captured and occupied Pondicherry. The Company's forces were now confidently aggressive and the Madras European Regiment was sent overseas. In February 1795 they garrisoned Bencoolen, in July they were part of the force engaging the Dutch in Ceylon. This island was subjugated by February 1796 and the army moved on against Malacca in the Dutch East Indies. Amboyna, Banda and Ternate were overrun and three new battle honours were credited to the Madras Europeans.

Because they were fully committed abroad the regiment did not play any great role in the last Mysore War. Ably planned by Lord Wellesley and executed with skill and determination by his officers, including his brother Sir Arthur Wellesley, the campaign against Mysore quickly culminated in the storming and capture of Seringapatam in May 1799. Tippoo died bravely defending his capital and with his death a bloody chapter of wars in south India came to an end.

It is inconceivable that John Stevenage did not take part in any of the numerous battles, sieges, actions and expeditions that occurred between his arrival in Madras in 1779 and the end of the wars with Mysore in 1799. There are many detailed accounts of the campaigns, many stirring stories of personal adventures, but no mention anywhere of John. Doubtless he played his small role in the great drama that the years unfolded and after repeated re- enlistments, retired from the army and settled down, probably in Tellicherry, the major British bastion on the Malabar coast. He was almost certainly recalled to play his part in the final struggle against Tippoo. But in April 1799, just before the decisive victory, he died, and the record of burials in the cemetery of St Mary's, Fort St George, Madras, states simply:

John Stevenage, Soldier, buried 8th April 1799

The fighting was over.

*The Arms, Colours, Accoutrements and
Trophies of the Regiment*

7

The Carnatic War Medal

Gold, Silver and Bronze medals were granted to all the Officers and Men who served during the Carnatic War.

Colonel R.E Wilson gives the following description of the Medal granted under the orders of the Governor General in Council – 22nd January 1785 – for service during the Carnatic War.

On one side is an inscription in Persian of which the following is a translation:

> The courage and exertions of those valiant men by whom the name of Englishmen has been celebrated and exalted from Hindustan to the Deccan, having been established throughout the world, this has been granted by the Government of Calcutta in commemoration of the excellent services of the brave. In the year of the Hegira 1199; year of Christ 1784.

On the obverse, the figure of Britannia seated apparently on Military Trophies and extending her right hand holding a wreath of laurel towards a Fort on which the British Colours are flying.

The Founding Of The Family

The Ecclesiastical Records section of the Oriental & India Office Collections in London, holds the returns of Baptisms, Marriages and Burials communicated by the church authorities in India. The oldest, dating from 1698, are from Madras but the whole series exhibits the same defects of incompleteness and error in transcription which characterise the bishops' transcripts of the ancient parish records of England.

Entries relating to the burial of John Stevenage are preserved both in London and in the local church records at Madras. The availability of any such record must be considered fortunate in circumstances where the British often died far away from the main settlements and formal Christian rites. The Indian soil holds many unmarked, unrecorded British graves. Local registers are greatly at risk from the climate, the ravages of insects and the carelessness of custodians. As a rule the Anglican clergy were meticulous in their records and abstracts, but the Catholic Missions, served by European and Indian priests, did not exhibit the same sense of responsibility or accuracy in this field. To make matters worse, even common British names took on some quite strange forms when recorded by foreigners.

No record of John's marriage is available in London nor has it been found in India. This is unfortunate but not surprising in the circumstances. The morals of the Europeans in India were not of the highest order and the hareems and plurality of wives enjoyed by the Indians did not help to raise the level of Christian public morality in this tropical clime. The number of European women of marriageable age was small and the chances of an unwise match were high. For the Europeans and more especially the British, marriage to an Indian woman or to the daughter of a domiciled French or Portuguese family was considered not only foolish but quite unnecessary. Certainly this was the 'official' view. Catholic marriages were held to be every bit as obnoxious as marriages with Indians. Was John one of those who did not bother with a marriage ceremony? Is the explanation simply that the record of his marriage was not forwarded to London and, if it has survived, still awaits discovery in some local church or dusty archive? Several straws point to a charitable conclusion.

Mylapore, or San Thome, stood just a mile to the south of Fort St George and provided Catholic Portuguese brides for generations of Englishmen from Madras. In the course of his army service there must have been ample opportunities for John to meet, woo and perhaps to wed, a French or Dutch or Danish maiden from the nearby foreign settlements. And of course, there were many eager young girls in Black Town, outside the north walls of the Fort. Here, marriages were often celebrated but not as often reported to the authorities. John's descendants were Catholics and this suggests a marriage in a Catholic church.

9

When the baptism certificate of John, son of John and Susanna is contrasted with frequent references in such documents to a 'natural child', the possibility of a legal marriage seems to grow.

The Asiatic Annual Register for 1799 has the following note:
> July 1798 – At a meeting of the European inhabitants of Madras, convened by the Sheriff, a subscription was proposed to be raised to be sent to England to help the War.

At the tail end of a long list of contributors over a period appears 'S.J Stevenage, 2 Pagodas'. At that time the only S. Stevenage known to be in India was the Susanna mentioned above – the mother of John Stevenage's son. Could it be that John's wife was an accepted member of the European community in Madras?

When John was recalled to the army for the final struggle against Tippoo Sultan, it would appear that Susanna remained at Tellicherry. Certainly her youngest child, John, was born there in May 1799. It must have been just about that time when she heard of the death of her husband at Madras, far away on the other coast. Warring armies would have made a dash across country unthinkable but Susanna hurried to Madras, probably braving the coastal voyage with all its dangers from the elements, pirates and the French navy. And she took her new born baby with her. She must have been too late to do more than visit her husband's grave and settle his affairs. But she did find the time to have the child baptised at Madras, calling him John after the father he would never see. Then she moved back to the west coast.

Susanna survived John by many years and the record of her burial which has survived, reads:
> Quilon, 2nd December 1834 – Susannah, relict of Serjeant John Stevenage, Madras Artillery aged about 90 years was buried by me G. Graeme, Chaplain, Archdeaconry of Madras.

Undoubtedly the age quoted was an exaggeration, but compared with the average life span of the Europeans in India, she must have seemed to have lived 90 years. The reference to the Madras Artillery is also confusing but would be appropriate if John had served the guns attached to his regiment. Although no military record ranks John as a Sergeant he was accorded this rank on the baptism certificate of his son, mentioned above. After about 20 years service it does not seem an unreasonable degree of promotion to assume.

The records of the East India Company do not show any other Stevenage going out to India or living there and so when the next generation of 'country born' Stevenages appear it is presumed that they are all the children of John.

John and Susanna had founded a family in India which was to grow in the next 200 years into a considerable clan. Indeed, every Stevenage since discovered can be traced back to this beginning. The name Stevenage had died out in England except as a location which was to be one of the earliest 'New Towns' in the United Kingdom.

St Mary's, Fort St. George

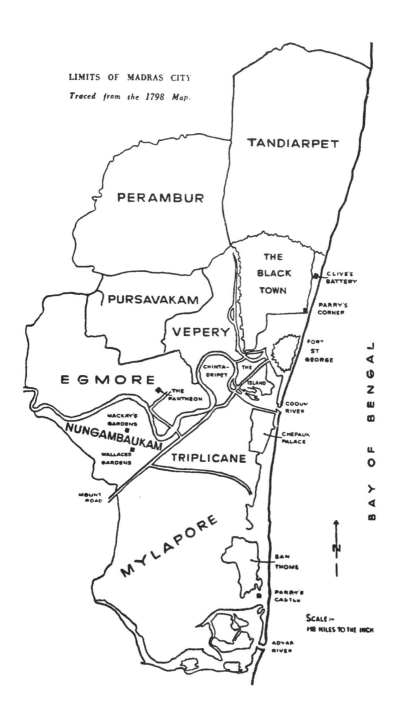

LIMITS OF MADRAS CITY
Traced from the 1798 Map.

TANDIARPET

PERAMBUR

THE
BLACK
TOWN

CLIVE'S
BATTERY

PARRY'S
CORNER

PURSAVAKAM

VEPERY

FORT
ST
GEORGE

CHINTA-
DRIPET

THE
ISLAND

EGMORE

THE
PANTHEON

COOUM
RIVER

MACKAY'S
GARDENS

CHEPAUK
PALACE

NUNGAMBAUKAM

WALLACES
GARDENS

TRIPLICANE

MOUNT
ROAD

MYLAPORE

SAN
THOME

N

PARRY'S
CASTLE

BAY OF BENGAL

SCALE :-
1½ MILES TO THE INCH

ADYAR
RIVER

Early Years In Madras

It was no easy task to bring up a family in Madras at the end of the 18th century. Society was sharply divided; on the one side there were the teeming masses of subject Indians; on the other side stood the rulers, the 'heaven born' representatives of the Company and the officers of the armies at first hired to protect trading ventures and latterly to carve out an empire within which the Company would enjoy preferential trading rights and exercise real powers of government. Yesterday's client traders overnight had become the rulers in India.

Between the two distinct societies of Europeans and Indians stood the twilight community of Anglo-Indians. They included families of pure European stock, 'country born' and domiciled in India; and also those of mixed descent through one or more generations of intermarriage. The range of their quality, education, culture and colour varied widely. Portuguese of pure European descent, in the third or fourth generations were often dark skinned in comparison with the offspring of successive generations of mixed marriages. Quality was measured by the economic resources of the family; education and culture were the products of environment and opportunity.

John Stevenage's family was part of the amorphous group of retired soldiers, subordinate clerks, petty traders and unsuccessful adventurers. Wealthy civil servants and officers could afford to send their legitimate and even their 'natural' children to be educated in England. Some princely Indian families were encouraged to follow suit. But an English education was out of the question for the children of John and Susanna. That they managed to acquire any education at all reflects great credit on their parents and probably, most on their mother. In Madras the parish school of St Mary's and the orphan asylums for boys and girls strove hard to provide an elementary education for a pitifully restricted number of children. In the *mofussil* there was nothing comparable. Reverend Swartz was one who realised the extent of the problem. In 1784 he reported to the Society for the Propagation of Christian Knowledge that the Anglo-Indian population of Madras and the Coromandel Coast was increasing by an estimated 700 per year and that in the absence of facilities for proper education and suitable employment they would soon pose a major problem. In some government circles this growth was viewed as a very real threat to the established order of things.

The French and the Dutch treated their creole and burgher families as equals in every respect, absorbed them into the system and found many opportunities to utilise their special advantages of kinship, language and sympathetic appreciation of local affairs. The British refused to acknowledge any liability in the situation they had created. Anglo-Indians, even those returning after an excellent English education, were not considered suitable for any position of real responsibility. The boys were started as drummers in the army or as petty clerks in commercial offices; the girls went into service as maids, nannies or seamstresses. Unless they were especially gifted they could not hope, even in a lifetime of service, to get very far along any road to success. Many vanished quickly into the native bazaars, brothels and thieves' dens. A few others, bolder spirits, deeply resenting real or imaginary injustices gravitated to the armies of the French, the Deccan rajas or the Mahratta princes. Here, they often won recognition for their talents, but to the English they were always 'renegades'. The British strongly disapproved of the Anglo-Indians and when they were of mixed blood described them as heirs to all the vices but none of the virtues of their forbears. The 'Indian Gazette' of 31st May 1792 reported that from that date Anglo-Indians were to be officially debarred from government service. Fortunately, this restriction did not endure.

It was against this background that four of the six sons of John Stevenage grew to maturity. Somewhere, somehow, they acquired an education and, despairing of a future in the now rigidly hierarchical settlement of Madras they struck out into new territory. The east coast was uninspiring, Mysore too recently a battlefield, but the west or Malabar coast with its forests, plantations and booming trade offered new and exciting prospects. Territories in this traditional gateway to India, recently freed from the domination of Mysore and brought within the ambit of British control became the first choice for the younger generation of Stevenages.

In the second half of the 18th century Travancore had emerged as the strongest power on the west coast. Her rulers had annexed Quilon and detached the support of the Dutch away from neighbouring Cochin and into their own camp. Never overrun by the armies of Mysore, Travancore joined the British in defensive alliances against Hyder Ali and Tippoo Sultan. Treaties followed and Travancore slipped quietly under British control, surrendering foreign policy and accepting limited interference in local affairs in exchange for British protection against all external enemies. The Maharaja of Travancore thus remained an almost independent ruler within the evolving British empire of India. He had his own government which administered law and order, local taxes, coinage, postage and all other internal affairs. This administration was carefully watched over by a benevolent British Resident who would be expected to intervene to correct serious misgovernment. But although the Native States accepted British Residents and British tutelage, they insisted on the freedom to run local government services with their own officials, recruited outside the direct control of the growing British bureaucracy. Anglo–Indians were welcomed in these state services for their own abilities and because they represented an acceptable minimal degree of Europeanisation. They identified more with the State and helped to gradually ease the traditional Indian way of life and government into a western pattern of relative efficiency and democracy.

An unfortunate manifestation of this spirit of local independence was that only the Anglican churches in the states of Travancore and Cochin made regular returns of entries in their registers to the authorities in British India and thence to London. Abstracts from the Registers of most Catholic churches in these areas were not forwarded and many of the original records have suffered irreparable damage or have been lost. Consequently, records of Stevenage baptisms, marriages and burials have been extremely hard to find and family traditions alone support some sections of the history of John's descendants.

John (John James) Stevenage

The youngest son of John and Susanna Stevenage is the best documented of all their family. His baptism certificate, his last Will and Testament and the inscription on his tomb all contribute to a reconstruction of his history. Additionally, he is mentioned in several books which chronicle his times.

John Stevenage was born in Tellicherry in May 1799, about a month after the death of his father in faraway Madras. He would not remember anything of the dash from Tellicherry when Susanna took her new-born son to Madras, probably to visit her husband's grave, to get a first hand account of his passing, and to settle his affairs. But this must have been an often repeated tale and the memory of it is hinted at in the inscription on his tomb. 'Born at Tellicherry: Baptised at Madras'. While she was at Madras, Susanna had the infant baptised. The record of baptism states that John, aged 5 months, the son of Sergeant John Stevenage and Susanna, was baptised at Vepery on 16th October 1799 by Mr Gericke, a missionary. At that time Vepery was a suburban military outpost of Fort St George and the Madras Artillery was quartered there.

Presumably Susanna and John returned to the west coast for the inscription on John's tombstone reads, 'Lived and Died at Cochin'.

Although no record of his marriage has been found, the monumental inscription records that he 'married Frances Cornelia Guzhlar'.

Manuel Gyselaar, his son 'Poney' Guizelaar and his grandson Cornelius Guizelaar, were all wealthy, successful shipbuilders at Cochin in a period when it supplied stout ships to Indian princes, European and Indian traders, the East India Company and even the Royal Navy. The names bestowed on the sons of John James and Frances Stevenage echo those of the older generations of Guizelaars.

It is not known whether John James was employed in the Guizelaar shipbuilding business or by the ruler of Cochin, but from his Will it is evident that he had acquired a more than modest fortune in his lifetime. One item mentioned was a property granted to him by the Maharaja of Cochin 'as Annobogom for ever', which would indicate his good standing at Court. The grant was set out on a bronze tablet which was carefully preserved by a Cochin landowner but, as recently as 1945, permission to view, photograph or copy this was not obtainable.

John James had his main residence at Mattoncherry, Cochin, and an extract from the *Church History of Travancore* by CM Agur shows that he was

15

fully involved in the religious strife which was endemic on the west coast where the conflict between Hindus and Muslims found a heated reflection in the arguments of the adherents of the Reformed Churches, the Roman Catholics and the Syrian Christians. An incident in the schism of 1838, when the relative authority of the Catholic Bishop of Cochin and the Vicar Apostolic of Malabar was in question, is related by the author of that monumental work: 'A few of the disaffected parishioners of Mattoncherry headed by one Mr Stevenage and his sons, formed themselves into a party and forwarded a memorial to the Vicar Apostolic acknowledging him as their prelate, who thereupon deputed Father Gregory de Santa Santisma Vergina the Carmelite Vicar of Chattiato, to proceed to Mattoncherry and receive the submission of the congregation there; but on the priest's arrival being opposed by the opposite party who had also memorialised their bishop and adopted timely measures to counteract them, Father Gregory could do no more than suspend their vicar Francisco Rodrigues Torres and place the church under interdict until matters could be further compromised. Meanwhile corpses were interred without funeral obsequies, children brought for christening were ordered to be taken back and the performance of Mass for the souls of the departed was omitted.'

But these disputes were over when John James, in his Will, provided 'Two hundred rupees, besides the 100 already given to Padre Sebastian Pereira during his existence, thus 300 rupees as a patrimony to any of the destitute student of clergyship at Verapoly during [their] life time and afterwards to be reverted again and again to another according to the discretion and option of the time being Bishop of Verapoly.'

John James had no doubt about his importance in the community. His Will enjoined that his executors, 'inter my body or corpse in a decent manner without any show or pomp, performing every day a Low Mass until the thirtieth day which should be celebrated also in a very low scale without grandeur on the same manner as that of the burial with the assistance not exceeding of five Padres.'

Back in 1843 his ego must have taken a severe knock in an incident recorded by TWVenn in his book *Cochin – Malabar: Palms and Pageants*. George Vernede was held up in his coach bandy at the Calvetti Bridge by John James Stevenage in a humbler vehicle. For this presumption George chastised John who, when he complained to Jean Scipion Vernede got the reply, 'It is lucky that he did not kill you for he is a powerful fellow.' It is doubtful that the matter ended there for Venn goes on to say that John James Stevenage was a person of some standing in his community. Venn also states that John James was buried under a substantial stone in the forecourt of Mattoncherry church. This clue led, eventually, to the uncovering of the grave before the door of Our Lady of Life church at Mattoncherry. The inscription on the tombstone provided valuable information to which reference has been made in the foregoing paragraphs.

Five of the children of John James and Frances Stevenage survived childhood and are mentioned in their father's Will, made shortly before his death in 1854. At that date the two daughters were married. Adelida Justina Roza and Leticia Brown received bequests which were additional to their marriage portions. Unfortunately the record of these marriages has not been found and no information is available about their husbands or their children if any. The only reference that has been turned up is to the death of Leticia Maria Brown, aged about 55 years, who died at Calicut on 26th October 1890. Nothing whatsoever has been found relating to Charles Stevenage, the second son, but Cornelio Augustus Stevenage, the eldest, and Peter Alcantra Stevenage, the youngest, have been traced and through them the line of John James Stevenage continues.

Because of their significance, the Will of John James Stevenage and the inscription on his tomb are reproduced here in full.

The Last Will And Testament Of John James Stevenage

I, the undersigned John James Stevenage being in bodily health and of sound and disposing memory, and considering the evils, dangers, and other uncertainties of this transitory life, do (for avoiding controversies after my death) make, publish and declare this my Last Will and Testament in manner following: that is to say,

First, I commend my soul to God, that gave it; and my body I commit to the earth or sea, as it shall please God to order:

And for and concerning all my worldly estate I give, bequeath and dispose thereof as followeth; that is to say,

First, I will that all my just debts and funeral charges be paid and discharged by my Executors hereinafter named:

I bequeath unto my eldest son Cornelio Augustus Stevenage to inherit my House situated in the town of Cochin in the Street denominated H as per Title Deed purchased from Mr Francis Snow, together with my House and Garden at Trichoor and all the cattle which are there.

Item   I bequeath unto my son Charles Stevenage to inherit the properties mortgaged to me by Kalicaren Tarrid Mopala of Ernacollum for interest in money and for 19 Chodanas of Oil annually with the accumulated interest until now together with all the materials which are already prepared for the building of a House.

Item   I bequeath unto my daughters Adelida Justina Roza and Leticia Brown my large House facing the Flagstaff in the Fort of Cochin bought from Mrs Snow to be equally divided or the income shared between them, having already given them their portions on their marriage as particularised in the enclosed Memo.

Item   I bequeath unto my youngest son Peter Stevenage my dwelling House and Compound at Mattoncherry granted to me by His Highness the Raja of Cochin as Annobogom for ever with all its appurtenances, Furnitures, Gold, Silver, Brass, Boats, Cattles and Chattels and everything else contained in the House or premises, as well as the Ground Rents, without removing a farthing, and for his support the land purchased in the tenure of Attiparr at Cuddawenthora in Ernacollum Proverty. All this to be enjoyed by him (Peter) when he attains the age of twenty or twenty one years, until which time I request his Mother and Brothers Cornelio and Charles will take care of him as Guardians, administer the property and give him good and liberal education.

Item   I bequeath unto my Grand-Son John James Stevenage a sum of one thousand Company's Rupees from having a particular love and regard for him, and from not having given his Father an equal sum as to his Sisters. This money should be given on compound interest and paid to him with the capital when he attains the age of twenty one years.

Item   I bequeath my House in the Kalver Street front of the Flagstaff bought from the estate of the late Mr Peter Winkler to my Grand-God-Daughter Gertruda Stevenage to be enjoyed by her and the rent or income derivable from it ought to be given out on compound interest and paid to her on her marriage.

Item   the income of the Garden which I have taken in mortgage from Blavelly Curtawo at Allengvonapella should be divided or shared by my three sons namely Cornelio, Charles and Peter.

Item   That it is my will and intention that my House and Garden at Chowarah should be enjoyed by my family i.e. my wife and her offspring, paying three rupees annually to the Curtawo from the produce of coffee.

Item   I bequeath two hundred (200) rupees, besides the one hundred already given to be enjoyed by Padre Sebastian Pereira during his existence thus (300) rupees as a Patrimony to any of the destitute student of clergyship at Verapoly during life time and afterwards to be reverted again and again to another according to the discretion and option of the time being Bishop of Verapoly.

Thank God I have no debt therefore all my outstandings ought to be recovered which with the ready cash contained in the accompanying List is left entirely to the disposal of my Wife and Sons.

Lastly I solemnly entreat and direct my Executors hereunder named will in due compliance with my earnest wish and request inter my body or corpse in a decent manner without any show or pomp, performing every day a Low Mass until the thirtieth day which should be celebrated also in a very low scale without grandeur on the same manner as that of the burial with the assistance not exceeding of five Padres.

This being my Last Will and Testament made with a clear conscience in discharge of my duty and obligation before God and Man, I trust that my Wife and Sons and Daughters will rest satisfied and contented with the same.

Nothing of this my aforesaid Will and disposition shall take effect or place during the life time of myself or my wife under whose sole control, careful management and administration every thing is left at present, after her death, which may Almighty God in his kind Providence long continue to preserve, the Surviving Executors of this my Testament will give due execution of the whole as above mentioned.

I request that a Packet which will be found amongst my papers may be delivered to my Brother Mr. H. B. Stevenage and slaves set free at liberty.

And I do hereby nominate, appoint and constitute my lawful wife and sons Cornelio and Charles as Executors and Administrators of this my Last Will and Testament, and hereby revoking all former the Wills and Testaments and Deeds of Gifts by me at any time heretofore made. And I do ordain and ratify these presents to stand and be for, as my Last Will and Testament.

In witness whereof, to this my said Will I have set my hand and seal at Cochin this ninth day of May in the year of our Lord one thousand eight hundred and fifty four.

(signed) Jno. J. Stevenage

Signed Sealed and Published and Delivered in the presence of, J.Pinto, J.P.Vernam, R.F.Freita, Jms.J.de Aranjo.

This Last Will and Testament (containing four lists and one Memo.) has been opened and read this day soon after the demise of the above mentioned Testator Mr. Jno. James Stevenage in the same room where his corps was deposited In witness whereof we hereunto set our hands.

Mattoncherry at Cochin this twelfth day of August 1854

I.V.Lobo, B.Guirelas, D.Gunther, L.de Padua

Notes:
1: The tenure of 'Annobogom' was the local equivalent of an entail which could only be broken by legal action and the Raja's consent.
2: Wherever a 'Garden' is mentioned it should be understood that it was the equivalent to an estate of indeterminate size for the growing of tea, coffee, spices, or coconuts.
3: The grandchildren mentioned, namely John James Stevenage and Gertruda Stevenage were the children of Cornelio Augustus Stevenage.

Monumental inscription on the tomb of John James Stevenage which stood before the front door of the Church of Our Lady Of Life, in Mattoncherry, Cochin (shown below).

SIN IS THE   CAUSE OF DEATH

TO
THE MEMORY
OF
JOHN JAMES STEVENAGE
BORN AT TELLICHERRY
BAPTISED AT MADRAS
MARRIED FRANCES
CORNELIA GUZHLAR
LIVED AND DIED AT COCHIN
THE 11 DAY OF AUGUST
A.D. 1854 AGED 55 YEARS
MAY HE REST IN PEACE

(In Malayalam)
CHRISTIAN PASSING THROUGH
PRAY FOR MERCY TO THE ALMIGHTY

(In Portuguese)
HOMOENS CATHOLICOS
PECO ENCARACIDAMENTE DEROGAR
A DEOS PARA SALVACO DESTE POBRE ALMA

Our Lady of Life – Mattoncherry

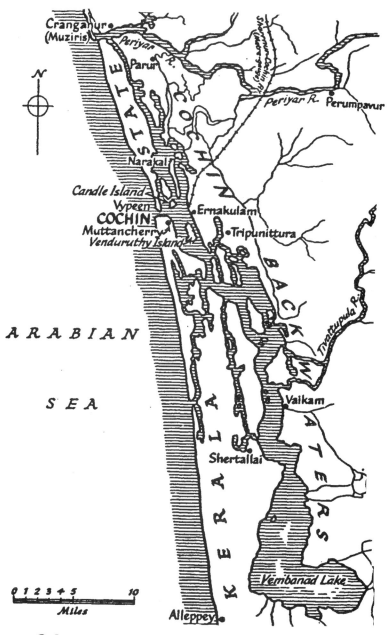

COCHIN & BACKWATERS

Santa Cruz Cathedral, COCHIN

22

The Stevenages Of Cochin

One branch of the Stevenage family settled in Cochin and continued there for about one hundred years. They lived mainly in the area of British Cochin but their property, interests and lives extended beyond the narrow enclave of Fort Cochin to Vypeen, Mattoncherry and Ernakulam in the State ruled by the Maharaja of Cochin.

Although Cochin was older, it was smaller and less 'progressive' than Travancore. It was known in history to the Phoenicians, the Egyptians, the Greeks, the Romans, the Chinese and the Jews. Pliny and Ptolemy disputed the exact position of the port of Muziris; the Romans left a temple to Augustus on its shores; the distinctive Chinese fishing nets are still to be seen around its fisheries; Jews settled in Cochin, Thomas the Apostle visited the area and founded the first Christian congregation there; the Syrian branch of the Catholic church established a flourishing See based on the Malabar coast. Then came the Muslims from Asia, Africa and nearby Mysore, who settled in a distinctive ethnic group called Moplahs. Last of all came the Europeans and this time the visitors were determined to stay and to rule the land. The Portuguese settled in Goa with Cochin as their second power base. They ruled the seas and a small area of the mainland from about 1500 until the advent of the Dutch around the middle of the 17th century. The Dutch ruled Cochin until the end of the 18th century. The French established a trading post at Mahé, but the tide flowed strongly in favour of the British. They proved strongest of all the Europeans both on the seas and on land. The Raja of Cochin, who had fallen under the rule of Tippoo Sultan's Mysore, just passed over power to the British when they defeated and killed Tippoo. The Dutch who had been neutral in the Mysore wars soon followed suit and surrendered their authority in Cochin to the British more under threat of force than the actual exercise of superior military and naval strength.

And so the land of spices, of dense forests and dark backwaters, the goal of so many adventuring foreigners, came under the suzerainty of the British who preserved the status of the raja but governed the country within that part of the expanding Indian empire that was classified as the Indian States. This land attracted a branch of the Stevenage clan.

Peter Alcantra Stevenage

In the second half of the 19th Century, Peter Alcantra, the youngest son of John James Stevenage, was the best known of the Stevenages of Cochin. He was born on 19th October 1835 but as the church in Mattoncherry was under interdict due to a religious controversy it is not known where he was baptised. He was still a minor when his father died in 1854 but he was handsomely provided for under the terms of his father's Will. John James specially requested that he

Church of Our Lady of Life, Mattoncherry

should be given a good and liberal education and should be under the guardianship of his mother and elder brothers until he achieved his full majority. In an era of arranged marriages, although he was 26 years of age at the time, it can be assumed that the family had a lot to do with the selection of his bride. The ancient family of Carvalho arrived in India with the early waves of Portuguese adventurers. They settled in the country and prospered greatly. This family provided suitably dowered brides for many important personages eg Charles Floyer II, a Member of the Council at Madras; Charles Smith who acted as Governor of Madras for a short time; M de Kerjean, the nephew of Governor Dupleix of Pondicherry; Jacques Law, Commander of the French Forces in South India; and Eustache de Lannoy, the Walloon who rose to command the armies of Travancore. Peter Alcantra's bride was Elizabeth Matilda Carvalho, the daughter of the Police Superintendent of Alwaye, Emmanuel Anton Carvalho and Gertrude Matilda his wife. She was born on 23rd August 1844 and the wedding took place in St Joseph's Cathedral, Trivandrum on 10th February 1862. The couple returned to live in Cochin where Elizabeth Matilda soon proved that she was an ideal wife – intelligent, an excellent housekeeper, a talented linguist, a careful manager of her husband's affairs and a fond mother to a rapidly growing family. She presented her husband at almost yearly intervals with sixteen children.

It may have been the necessity of providing for this family or it could have been the inevitable result of his good education but Peter Alcantra entered the service of the Maharaja of Cochin and rose rapidly. In this he probably had some help from his cousin Francis Rice who was then the Secretary of the English Department of the State Government. His career can be seen from a study of the successive issues of the *Madras Almanac* and *Thacker's Indian Directory*:

   1875   Head Writer, Huzoor English Department, Cochin State
   1876   Acting Accountant, English Department, Cochin State
   1877   Accountant, English Department, Cochin State
   1880   Head Clerk, English Department, Cochin State
   1891   Manager, English Department, Cochin State

The last entry of his service relates to 1895 and it is presumed that he retired when he reached the age of 60 years.

It can be assumed that Peter earned a good wage to add to the income from the property left to him by his father. It was the custom of the Maharaja to reward good service with occasional gifts of money and more often with grants of land and in this manner Peter prospered greatly. Perhaps things came too easily to him, his children confess that he was a heavy drinker and he never drank alone. It was well known that at a suitable stage of his 'entertaining' he could be persuaded to present his friends and cronies with the titles to small parcels of land or the rents from his properties. This proved to be quite expensive and wealth flowed out as fast as it flowed in. Fortunately Elizabeth Matilda took steps to hide away some of the property deeds and in any case he could not part with the entailed property he inherited from his father. But when, in due course, Peter came to make his Will he could not claim, as his father had done, that he left no debts.

Of the sixteen children born to Matilda and Peter ten survived the perils of childhood in the tropics and arrived at a healthy maturity. One of the girls, blessed with a sound memory, many years later recounted the roll call of the children and their birthdays. Such data as has come to light confirms the accuracy of her memory. The children were:-

Frances Gertrude	born 1863 (died young)
Charlotte Marian	born 23rd February 1864
Josephine Maria	born 2nd April 1865
Alvaris	(died young)
Mary Jane	born 25th June 1867
Catherine Adelaide	born 23rd March 1868
John James	born 5th October 1869
Joseph Patrick	born 11th October 1871
Maurice	(died young)
Anne Emily	(died young)
Gertrude Maria	born 10th September 1875
Emanuel Antony	born 20th December 1877
Charles Leo	born 25th February 1879 (died young)
Henrietta Imelda	born 6th December 1880
Francis Xavier	born 9th July 1883 (died young)
Anna Elizabeth	born 30th March 1886

When Peter Alcantra died early in 1900, he was obviously concerned for the future of his unmarried daughters but only one of them died an old maid. The others, profiting from their father's estate, married and lived in reasonable affluence. All his surviving children are mentioned in the will of Peter Alcantra which is reproduced below in full.

The Last Will And Testament Of Peter Alcantra Stevenage

Know all men by these presents, that I, Peter Alcantra Stevenage, being by the Grace of God of sound mind and understanding, do hereby make, publish and declare this my Last Will and Testament in revocation of all former ones.

In order to make due provision for my family consisting of my wife, Elizabeth Matilda, four unmarried daughters, Catherine Adelaide, Gertrude Maria, Henrietta Imelda and Elizabeth Anne, and three sons, Joseph Patrick, John James and Emanuel Antony, I hereby make the following disposition of my property.

1   As I have on the 19th January 1900, given to my wife, Elizabeth Matilda, by Deed of Gift my dwelling house in No.4 Napier Street as per Municipal Register, the said house is absolutely at her disposal.

2   The furniture that I may die possessed of and the silver ware shall be in the common enjoyment of my heirs; but my executors shall be at liberty to dispose of all or any portion of the same to meet any urgent necessity.

3 Of the properties belonging to me in the Cochin State, Cochin Poverty, Mattencherry District and specified in the Teetoorom of Kaikadogom 1050 granted to me by His Highness the Maharajah of Cochin under the tenure of Annubogam for ever, one portion is now in my possession and the rest including the two bungalows which were repaired and constructed from bankshalls, as will be seen from the Teetoorom, together with the reclaimed portion of land on the Eastern side of the Annubogam property which is registered in my name under the tenure of Pandara Puthuvel Veroompattam, are given on pattom or rent by me and am in receipt of the rents thereof.

4   As the Annubogam properties can not be sold or mortgaged by virtue of the Teetoorom, I enjoin on my executors not to dispose of the land in any manner so as to depreciate the value of the said properties. Subject to this condition however, they are at liberty to dispose of the same.

5   I hereby enjoin that the rents of my property given on lease and the income of my property in my possession shall be collected and after paying taxes and the interest on my debts, be devoted to the common support of my wife, unmarried daughters and my sons.

6   I further enjoin that the said income shall be administered by my wife, Elizabeth Matilda, according to her own discretion and judgement and without any interference from the other heirs.

7   Should by dispensation of Providence my married daughters Charlotte Marian Lafrenais and Josephine Maria Platel, or any other of my daughters who may hereafter be married, be rendered widowed or destitute, the said daughter or daughters shall be entitled to support in case she or they come to reside in the common family house. I further direct that the sum of Rupees (15) fifteen per annum be given to my daughter Mary Jane who has taken the veil, and is known as Sister Agnes of the S.H.J. during her life for her clothing.

8   I hereby nominate, appoint and constitute my wife Elizabeth Matilda, my son-in-law, Charles William Lafrenais and my son John James as my Executrix and Executors respectively of this my Last Will and Testament. In the unavoidable absence of any one of them from the Station, the remaining two are hereby empowered to act under the Will.

9   I enjoin on my executrix and executors to liquidate my debts when they fall due by raising funds according to their discretion provided they shall not in any wise raise loans chargeable on my property except to discharge my lawful debts.

10   If at any time it is found imperative to transfer the Tax Registry name of my reclaimed lands or to renew the Teetoorom on which my Annubogam properties are held I authorise one of my then surviving sons to do so in his name with the assent of the other heirs. Nevertheless the son in whose name the transfer may be made and the Teetoorom may be renewed shall not on any account obtain any special right or claim over the property and shall not himself deal in any way with the property without the consent of all other heirs, executrix and executors.

11   In the event of one or more of the Executrix and the two Executors dying the survivor or survivors are empowered to nominate their successors. 12 Receipts for the rents of my properties shall be given by my wife Elizabeth Matilda during her life time and thereafter by one of my sons or eldest unmarried daughter.

12   My funeral expenses shall be defrayed according to the discretion of my Executrix and Executors in a quiet and unostentatious manner.

13   With an earnest exhortation to my wife and children to live in the fear of God and peace and concord among themselves, I conclude this my Last Will and Testament, by subscribing my signature and setting my hand and Seal in the presence of the undersigned witnesses on this 20th day of January in the year of our Lord one thousand nine hundred.

(signed) P.A. Stevenage

Witnesses:
1   M. Augustus
2   Wm. Chas. Carvalho
(The will bears the faint trace of a seal and is endorsed in the top right hand corner of the first page with initials and the date 22/5/00).

After the death of Peter Alcantra, his widow and the executors of his will got a law passed in the Cochin Legislature permitting them to by-pass the entail on his Annubogam property. It is not known in whose name the property was registered before its eventual sale but it certainly was not in the name of Emanuel Antony, his youngest surviving son. Elizabeth Matilda settled Peter's estate and then retired to the convent in Ernakulam where her daughter was a nun. She died there on 15th September 1918. Her will reads as follows:

Dated 24th August 1906

Will Of Elizabeth Matilda Stevenage

I, Elizabeth Matilda Stevenage, widow of the late Peter Alcantra Stevenage of Cochin declare this to be my Last Will.

I appoint Joseph Patrick Stevenage, John James Stevenage, Emanuel Antony Stevenage, my sons, and Charles William Lafrenais, my son-in-law, to be the Executors and Trustees of this my Will.

And I hereby devise and bequeath all my real and personal estate unto my said Executors in trust for my heirs; provided always and I declare that my said Executors shall have power to sell any of my properties if and as they shall deem fit and to hold the proceeds in trust as aforesaid.

(signed) E.M. Stevenage

Signed and acknowledged by the above named Elizabeth Matilda Stevenage as her Will in the presence of us present at the same time, who, in her presence, and in the presence of each other, have hereunder subscribed our names as witnesses.

(Signed) A.E. Pinto, J. Isaaks

In accordance with the clear wishes of their parents and taking into account the relative financial position of the sons and unmarried daughters, John James, Joseph Patrick and Emanuel Antony gave up most, if not all, of their claims to benefit under these Wills in favour of their unmarried sisters.

29

Helena Augusta Stevenage (the author's mother) c1901

The author's parents on their wedding day at Guntakal

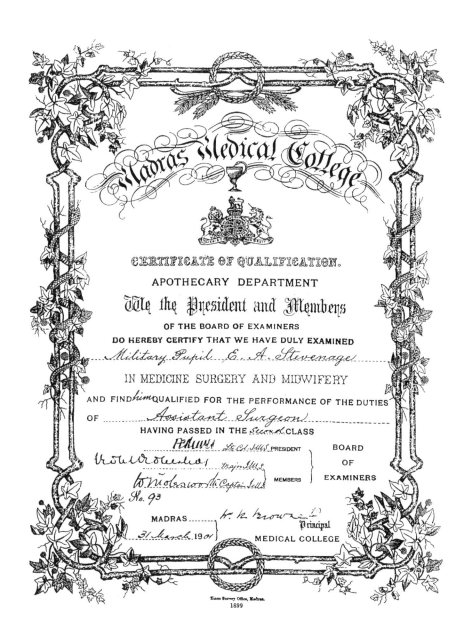

Emanuel Antony Stevenage's Certificate of Qualification, 1901

32

Emanuel Antony Stevenage

The youngest surviving son of Peter Alcantra mentioned in his Will was Emanuel Antony. He was born in Cochin on 20th December 1877 and educated at Santa Cruz High School, Cochin. When he decided that he wanted to be a doctor and to join the Madras Medical School as a military pupil he found that he was one year over the maximum prescribed age limit. In those days this was not an insuperable obstacle and he managed to convince the authorities that he was born on 20th December 1878. He got a place in the Medical School, passed all his examinations, and qualified as an Assistant Surgeon in the Indian Medical Department. All his records in the Medical School and in the Army show 1878 as his accepted date of birth. Perhaps as a consequence of this piece of deception all subsequent efforts to secure a copy of his baptism certificate (which serves in lieu of a birth certificate in India) have proved unavailing.

A brief summary of the Army career of Emanuel Antony Stevenage can be culled from the Indian Army Lists:

31st March 1901	Joined the Indian Subordinate Medical Dept. Assistant Surgeon 4th Class
31st March 1906	Assistant Surgeon 3rd Class
31st March 1913	Assistant Surgeon 2nd Class
1st October 1917	Assistant Surgeon 1st Class
1st January 1927	Commissioned as Lieutenant Senior Assistant Surgeon
27th January 1932	Captain Senior Assistant Surgeon
1st November 1933	Retired

It is obvious that promotion was strictly on the basis of years of service. Except for a spell on the North West Frontier, Emanuel did not see active service. A tour of duty on the frontier was always exciting because of the continuous tension with the tribes which could flare suddenly with a bout of sniping, a few dead or wounded, a punitive action by the army, and then back to the uneasy truce. Emanuel Antony used to relate to his children the usual tales of fearsome tribesmen, their cunning raids on army outposts and the seeming ease with which they vanished into their hills. But none of these tales were related in the first person although he did do his turns of duty in the furthest outposts – Dera Ismail Khan, Landi Kotal, Bannu and Kohat.

Before he went to the frontier, Emanuel Antony Stevenage had spent a short time as the Medical Officer in the prisoner-of-war camp for the Boer prisoners at Bellary. While he was there he met, wooed and married Helena Augusta Rylands, the youngest daughter of Michael Norman Rylands, the railway doctor stationed at the nearby Railway Headquarters of Guntakal. The wedding took place on 18th February 1903 in the little church of St Ann at Guntakal. Many years later when their youngest son Patrick Hugh was stationed at Guntakal, the parish priest presented him with a letter written by his father requesting a copy of his marriage lines which he wanted to place on record with the authorities.

Helena was not allowed further than the large military centre of Quetta where she loved the shows, the parties and the generally gay life. Her two eldest children, Leonard Peter (26th January 1904) and Norman Valentine Mervin (31st August 1908) were born in Quetta. She often claimed that the boys learned Pushtu from the servants before they mastered English. The whole family were a bit sorry when, after five years on the frontier they were ordered south. The birthplaces of another five children mark the army stations at which Emanuel Antony was stationed over the years that followed:

> Joseph Antony born at Belgaum on 20th August 1910
> Phyllis Marjorie Helena born at Kirkee on 2nd November 1912
> Theresa Beryl born at Secunderabad on 27th June 1914
> Viola Ann born at Secunderabad on 28th May 1917
> Patrick Hugh born at Bangalore on 7th June 1922

With the outbreak of World War I, Emanuel Antony volunteered for service abroad and although he repeated this several times, the powers-that-be had decided that he would be doing the most good training the large numbers of recruits that flooded into the ranks of the army Bearer Corps. For this work, Emanuel had the special qualification of the gift of tongues. He read, wrote and spoke fluent Malayalam, Tamil, Telegu, Canarese and Gujarati. This was in addition to Dutch, Persian, Pushtu and the frontier dialects he acquired while he was on the frontier. In those days the army paid a bounty for each language in which an officer qualified and with a growing family, Emanuel was keen to increase his income as much as his knowledge. At any rate he was able to teach the raw recruits the elements of their duties in their own language and this was what the army wanted. So Emanuel Antony stayed in Secunderabad for the duration of the war, he did not collect any campaign medals but in due course, perhaps as a consolation, he acquired a good conduct medal.

Thacker's *Indian Directory* and the *Madras Almanac* track his movements:

> 1902 Belgaum
> 1903 Bellary
> 1904 Quetta
> 1909 Belgaum
> 1912 Kirkee
> 1914 Secunderabad: army Bearer Corps
> 1922 Bangalore
> 1922 Madras: on loan to the Civil Department

Resident Medical Officer, Govt Hospital, Royapuram Lecturer, Stanley
Medical School, Madras
1931   Assistant Port Health Officer, Madras
1933   Reverted to the Military: Bangalore

The three eldest boys were educated in St Joseph's College, Bangalore and
when their parents moved into a more settled existence in the Civil Medical
Department at Madras, the girls went to the local convents, and the two younger
girls, in due course, were packed off as boarders in the convent at Yercaud in
the Sheveroy Hills. Helena insisted that her youngest child Patrick should be
kept near her and so he was educated in Madras.

This was a happy time for the Stevenage family. Joseph Patrick and his
family had settled in Perambur; his sisters Josephine Maria Platel and Gertrude
Maria Carvalho also lived in Madras. Emanuel Antony's family joined this
growing clan. As the children finished their schooling they went into the medical colleges or the teachers training and commercial colleges; they joined the
railway companies and took apprenticeships in the various large engineering
companies which were growing up in Madras. The family religiously forgath-
ered at Christmas time and for birthdays; they holidayed together – going on
pilgrimage to Velankanni, on picnics at Ennore and on holidays to Ootacamund
and above all to Bangalore, where they joined up with the other branches of the
family happily settled there.

Emanuel Antony was essentially a family man; he was quiet and unas-
suming and was never known to lose his temper with his family or his staff, no
matter how great the provocation. His work was demanding but received priority over all considerations of self. He seemed to be always available to perform
operations, answer sick calls or take his boat out to a ship wallowing in the
rough surf of Madras and demanding medical attention for an injured or sick
crewman. It was understandable that he was loved and respected by all. Despite
the many calls on his time Emanuel Antony managed to fit into his schedule
long weekend sessions of bridge and even longer 'post mortems' after each
closely fought hand. He played tennis and billiards and took part in organising
many of the functions in the local departmental clubs. Helena Augusta, with
her usual energy, threw herself into everything that was happening around her.
A regular at the club she too played tennis and billiards, danced quite a lot, and
was present at most of the parties and concerts that were part of the round of
local entertainment. But her first concern was always the welfare of her children. Although she ruled them firmly they all knew that they could turn to her
with their problems and be certain of her sympathy and even more important,
of her help. The younger generations of the other branches of the family soon
realised the advantages of her approachability and her willingness to help wherever possible. A friend at the 'family court' was an important asset. Childish

ailments, school problems, afflictions of the heart, career difficulties; they all came to her for solution or alleviation. Never once was she found wanting or unhelpful even with the most taxing appeals for help from her children, their cousins and in due course the next generation whose attitudes were even more akin to her way of thinking.

Retirement was not to be a time of comfortable good health and ease. Emanuel Antony suffered a stroke of paralysis on the eve of his retirement from the army. This put paid to all his plans to settle down in the house that he had bought on St John's Hill, Bangalore, close to his sisters. The climate did not seem to suit him and the children were all back in Madras, so he decided to return there. As the years passed he seemed to recover a good deal of mobility. But the first stroke was followed by a second and then a third, fatal, stroke. He died peacefully in the garden of his home in Royapuram on 6th April 1941 and was laid to rest in the cemetery of St Rocque.

Memorial Inscription

IN SAD AND EVER LOVING MEMORY
OF
MY BELOVED HUSBAND AND OUR DARLING DAD
CAPT. EMMANUAL ANTHONY STEVENAGE
WHO PASSED AWAY PEACEFULLY ON THE 26th APRIL 1941
AGED 62 YEARS AND 3 MONTHS
SADLY MISSED AND DEEPLY MOURNED
NOT JUST TODAY BUT EVERY DAY
IN SILENCE WE REMEMBER

After the death of her husband, Helena Augusta seemed to surrender the battle against her own failing health. She had long suffered from chronic cardiac asthma but till now had resisted its impact upon her life and many activities. She retired into her shell and spent more and more of her time in bed. All her children, except the youngest son, had married and left home and it was her family doctor's considered verdict that Mrs Stevenage would only get well when one of her children became sick or in some other way demanded her active help and intervention. It was not illness in the family that finally aroused her spirits but the more vital impact of Indian Independence upon them and their future lives. As her doctor had correctly diagnosed, her will was always stronger than any ailment. She arranged her affairs in India and determinedly marched up the gangway of the ship which was to bring her from Bombay to the England she had never seen, but which she confidently expected would offer the best future for her children. Her eldest son Leonard and his family had preceded her; her second son Norman Valentine accompanied his mother and one by one all the other children followed. She argued, pleaded with and bullied each one in turn, and where she, a frail old lady could lead, how could they resist following her? The snow and ice of a wintry England reminded her of her youth in Quetta, people responded to her friendliness and she seemed to recover some of her health and good spirits. But when the family were all safely settled in the promised land she slipped back again. She lived with her sons, mostly with Norman Valentine, but found time to visit her daughter Theresa. On one such visit, she slipped and fell and broke her leg and while making a slow recovery in hospital, she suffered a cerebral thrombosis and died in Croydon on 22nd October 1963. So passed a grand old lady, the mother of her clan. She was buried in Elmer's End Cemetery, Norwood, and the stone over her grave reads:

IN
LOVING MEMORY OF
OUR DEAREST MOTHER
HELENA AUGUSTA STEVENAGE
BORN 31st MAY 1884 – DIED 22nd October 1963
MAY SHE REST IN PEACE

Your loving mother

The author's mother in England c1950

The Stevenages In Bangalore

Towards the end of the 19th century the Stevenages began to drift from the west coast to Bangalore, a civil and military station situated in the middle of Mysore State.

The reasons why so many of the Stevenages settled in Bangalore are not hard to find. The town, perched almost 3500 feet above the plains of the Carnatic, offered the sort of climate that has often been described as 'England in spring and summer all the year round'. Its air was cool and bracing, perfect for a holiday or recuperation after illness or a long hard stint in the constant heat and dust of south India. Everybody visited Bangalore at one time or another and seemed to remember it with affection and a smile for happy days well spent. For those who lived there it was the perfect home for retirement.

In the civil and military station, or cantonment area, people lived in large bungalows set in well-stocked gardens where flowers and flowering shrubs filled every little space without any apparent plan or design except to produce a riot of colour to satisfy the *mali's* eye. Trained servants were easily acquired and relatively inexpensive. The market stalls overflowed with every variety of fruit, vegetable, meat, poultry and game. The shops along the South Parade, in Commercial Street and on Brigade Road, were packed with European goods, imported to cater for a large community whose culture and taste was completely British. Bangalore still had a large garrison of European troops and once they had experienced its advantages, many servicemen returned there to live out their retirement in pleasant comfort. At one time there were no fewer than fifteen colonels and correspondingly higher numbers of majors and captains settled in Bangalore.

Inevitably, such a community demanded good clubs, theatres, cinemas and large well-kept parks, complete with painted bandstands where regimental bands played regularly to politely circling audiences. In the summer there was a short season of flat-racing on the beautiful racecourse. All year round there was good shooting to be found in the surrounding forests of Mysore; deer, wild pig, panthers and even tigers. In town there was plenty of scope for exercise, riding around the Parade Ground, polo, golf, tennis, cricket, hockey, soccer and even rugby when the ground grew softer in winter. This was a relatively affluent community which could afford the better things in life, and still carefully keep within their means. The convents, schools and colleges provided a European education for the younger generation of the residents and for the children of those families whose jobs held them on the plains of the south and who could not afford to send their offspring back to England to be educated. Bangalore was conveniently near and they could hope to escape there every now and then for a glorious holiday and family reunion. By tacit agreement the residents backed into their comfortable shells in the summer holiday season and 'lent' their beautiful town and often part of their homes, to the visitors.

Bangalore seemed to be the playground of the prettiest girls and there were always suitable partners to be found for tennis, a club dance, visits to the local cinema, or just for a stroll around the shaded walks of Cubbon Park or the Lal Bagh. In the first half of the 20th century, before World War II brought the Aircraft Factory and some light industry to the area, there was little to hold the young people in search of a career and they drifted away to Madras or Bombay in search of higher education, technical training and a job with prospects.

But more than anything else, Bangalore was a military centre where the regular garrison was boosted in war-time by huge rest and rehabilitation camps, and where the Officers Training College and the prisoner-of-war camps occupied large areas just outside the town. Bangalore expanded during the wars, it took to its heart the growing armies of British and Indian troops, trained them and sent them out to fight and then later, received back the sick, the wounded, the war-weary, and healed them in body and in spirit.

Bangalore was undoubtedly the 'Queen of the Hill Stations' and in the idyllic years between 1900 and 1950 it became the home of many of the Stevenages, a well-remembered place for romances and happy holidays and for some a beloved birthplace whose memory was always dear. But the time of reckoning had to come and when the end of World War II heralded the dawn of Indian Independence, the Stevenages packed their bags in Bangalore as in all other places in India and faced the test of a return to the land of their ancestors, a very different land if compared with that from which John Stevenage had departed in 1777.

The End Of The British Empire In India

On 15th August 1947 the Labour Government in Britain gave India its Independence and Pakistan its beginning. With the surrender of the 'Jewel in the Crown' the British Empire began to crumble. Lord Louis Mountbatten, the cousin of King George VI, had been appointed Viceroy of India and took up this post with the firm intention of carrying out the Government's mandate and bringing the job to a speedy conclusion. His determination to keep to his self-imposed timetable was to cost the lives of many hundreds of thousands, maybe even millions, of the population. Everybody who knew India and its peoples realised that Hindus and Muslims were just waiting for the removal of British power to spring into deadly action and slaughter one another. But the timetable was to be supreme and the only apparent regret of its author was that he was not invited to become President, both of the new India and the new Pakistan. The advice he gave the princes of India, bound to the Crown by long-standing loyalties and treaties, was that as the cousin of the King it was his recommendation that they should surrender their ancient rights and make whatever deals they could with the new governments. They did, and bitterly rued the day they yielded their hereditary rights and even their personal fortunes into the hands of greedy politicians.

The Anglo–Indian population of India had never believed that they would ever witness the end of British rule in India. To them it was something so far in the future that nobody seemed to clearly face up to such a future. To any suggestion that they should become fully Indianised the answer was an indignant 'Never'. They were Christians not Hindus or Muslims, Jains or Buddhists. English was their mother-tongue; they dressed in European fashion; they went to superior schools and served the government in many reserved occupations in the Post and Telegraph Departments and on the railways; their ancestors had formed the backbone of the regiments, both British and Indian, which had conquered India and fought in so many of the wars of Empire with more than a little distinction. No, they could never be just another Indian community. If the British left India they too must go. Where? Anywhere.

At first the residual authorities of the British Government in India tried to help the Anglo-Indians to leave. They were given assisted passages and temporary documentation, and in many cases where British descent could be proved, however slightly, British passports were readily handed out. But in due course the rules were tightened, it became harder, if not impossible, for savings, pensions and personal fortunes to be taken out of India. British passports were harder to obtain and the Anglo-Indians had to turn to other Commonwealth countries such as Australia, which still operated an 'open-door' policy.

The Anglo-Indian population in India was never under any illusion as to how the new governments would treat them. Certainly Anglo-Indians were never physically attacked. As long as they could not be replaced overnight by suitably trained Indians they would be tolerated, but promotion was quite another matter. Some Anglo-Indians were retained to serve in the armed forces, particularly in the air force and the navy. They also had a continuing role to play on the railways and in the telegraph offices. But clerical and administrative jobs were for the Indians and the Pakistanis. The police and the judiciary were sensitive positions and they were readily recognised as the perks of political parties and politicians. As the years passed, the better elements of the community vanished from the scene. Those who remained, mostly because they could not afford to get out or had left it too late, found that they had become a 'depressed class' in every sense.

But the Stevenages did not wait to be pushed out or depressed, they were among the first to quit the shores of the country where they had lived happily, prosperously and usefully for more than four generations, nearly two hundred years.

It will have been noted from the previous sections of this record that the Stevenage girls found it easy to slip away from their birthplace and to be absorbed into the culture and life of new homelands. From the fifth generation of the descendants of John Stevenage of Surrey three girls settled in the United States of America, one in Switzerland, one in Sweden and one in Italy.

The Stevenages settled in greater numbers in Australia and England and one family even made a home in Rhodesia.

The story of the Stevenages is picked up in the autobiography of Patrick Hugh Stevenage, the great-great-grandson of John Stevenage with whom this narrative began.

Part II - My Own Story

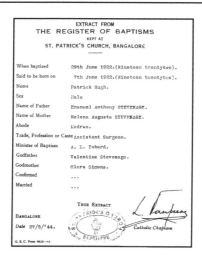

EXTRACT FROM
THE REGISTER OF BAPTISMS
KEPT AT
ST. PATRICK'S CHURCH, BANGALORE

When baptized	29th June 1922.(Nineteen twentytwo).
Said to be born on	7th June 1922.(Nineteen twentytwo).
Name	Patrick Hugh.
Sex	Male
Name of Father	Emanuel Anthony STEVENAGE.
Name of Mother	Helena Augusta STEVENAGE.
Abode	Madras.
Trade, Profession or Caste	Assistant Surgeon.
Minister of Baptism	A. M. Tabard.
Godfather	Valentine Stevenage.
Godmother	Clara Simons.
Confirmed	...
Married	...

TRUE EXTRACT

BANGALORE

Date 27/5/'44.

Catholic Chaplain

G. S. C. Press 9632—43

St. Patrick's Cathedral, Bangalore

43

The author's mother in fancy dress at Bangalore in 1922

Early Memories

My family has often suggested that I should write a detailed account of my life and as I am a student of genealogy and have in my possession almost every piece of paper necessary to make my story both factual and complete I feel that the time has come to commence the task.

In India, British subjects of European descent do not as a rule have birth certificates, they rely on baptism certificates which in due course find their way into the records of the Registrar General of Births, Marriages and Deaths in India and thence to the Oriental and India Office Collections in London from whom an impressive sealed document may be obtained on payment of the appropriate fee.

My baptism certificate shows that I was baptised on 29th June 1922, by Revd Father AM Tabard in St. Patrick's Roman Catholic cathedral at Bangalore in the Madras Presidency, south India. The certificate states that I was said to have been born on 7th June 1922, that I was a male child named Patrick Hugh, that my mother's name was Helena Augusta Stevenage, that my father was Emanuel Anthony Stevenage, an Assistant Surgeon, and that my parents were resident at Madras. My god-parents were Valentine Stevenage (my elder brother) and Clara Simons (of whom I know nothing). This document has served to identify me satisfactorily to every person or authority that has required such an identification.

My mother told me that I was a very considerate child, who arrived in the Bowring Hospital, Bangalore sometime between 3pm and 5pm which gave her time to get back from the delivery room to her bed and to make herself, and me, presentable to visitors who surely included my three sisters, Phyllis (aged ten), Theresa (aged eight), and Viola (aged five). I expect my brothers Leonard, Valentine and Joseph also made an appearance on this momentous occasion – there would have been a loud protest from mother if they did not. Dad was excused as he was a few hundred miles away working in the Royapuram General Hospital and so he had to wait a while to see me.

The seventh child is supposed to be lucky and mother once told me that when she was expecting her third, and feeling rather down at the prospect, a dear old priest blessed her and said that God would always send her a sort of compensation with every child, not only the babe itself but something more tangible. She claimed that this proved true and in due course the compensation for me arrived, perhaps a bit late, when in 1923 Dad was promoted as resident Medical Officer of the Royapuram General Hospital. In January 1927, he was promoted again to senior assistant surgeon and commissioned as a lieutenant in the Indian Medical Department – but that had nothing to do with me.

My first memories of a home are of the RMO's quarters alongside the hospital at Royapuram. It still seems huge in my memory, plenty of rooms and a garden with mango trees, everything a little boy could wish for. My eldest brother Len was my favourite. He taught me to play hockey and cricket, how to manage a hockey stick and a cricket bat and to bowl spinners, even a 'chinaman'- I still don't know what a chinaman is supposed to do with a cricket ball but it all sounded terribly impressive to my friends. He took me to see boxing and wrestling matches and when we got home he showed me how to take off my shoes, tie the laces around my neck and creep up the stairs so that I would not waken my parents – what a hope! Viola, the youngest of my sisters was a regular tomboy, she played marbles with me and my friends, climbed trees even higher than we dared to venture, and joined in all our games. Mine was a happy childhood pampered and loved by my large family and this state of affairs continued and became even more important when I started school. I fear that my mother spoiled me more than a bit and my *ayah*, Kistamah, was even worse, she even came between us on the very few occasions that mother tried to smack me or take her hairbrush to my bottom. She told me bedtime stories in high-class Tamil from the Ramayana and the Mahabharata, and it was from her that I received a good grounding in the language of south India. The stories themselves were as exciting as any western fairy tale and long enough to keep me awake for those important extra minutes before sleep finally took over.

Whenever people think of India they think of the luxury of having servants. We had the usual quota, a cook; a little boy or girl (*chokra* or *chokree*) to help around the house and kitchen and generally to run errands; a driver (he was nothing so posh as a chauffeur); a baby's *ayah* (Kistamah was my *ayah*); an indoors sweeper; a sweeper who kept the bathroom and the usual thunderboxes clean at all times; a *dhobi* who visited us once a week and took away a mountain of laundry to be washed, sometimes beaten to shreds, and eventually to be brought back immaculately starched and ironed; and a butler. Solomon our butler was a large, impressive figure of a man who never seemed to do anything very much. When Dad's good conduct medal vanished and a bright new 'S' appeared in Solomon's turban it was decided that we could well do without the services of a butler. The hospital provided gardeners and a host of bearers who appeared almost miraculously whenever they were needed. The establishment was reduced when we moved to a smaller house but basically we had the same sort of services performed for us.

Our servants were a sort of clan who gathered around us, each one jealous of his or her position, rights and responsibilities. When any of them fell sick we arranged medical treatment; when other assistance was needed they readily turned to us for help, and we did help. This sort of protection and insurance was extended to their families as a matter of course. If they went on leave they arranged for a relative to cover their duties. They claimed the right to enjoy all our happy occasions, birthdays, weddings, Christmas, and New Year. My birthday became the day when I presented my *ayah* with a gift, usually a new sari. The other servants similarly expected, and received, gifts at Christmas or the New Year. In return we received their affection and undying loyalty.

Servants were essential to our lives in India but they were also in many ways our responsibility.

Health seems to be one of the worries when people think of life in the tropics. As a child I suffered a bout of malaria almost every month but Dad prescribed an ounce of quinine daily and taken with a sweet it became almost endurable. At any rate my attacks of malaria vanished when I was about eight years old and the treatment was discontinued. Mother always seemed to think that I had a weak chest, but other than the usual colds and coughs there was no evidence to enhance her fears. Acting on the basis that prevention was better than cure, I was dosed regularly with Virol, rubbed down with cod-liver oil till my vests stank of the stuff, and when shark-liver oil became popular Mother tried to dose me with that, but this time I firmly said 'nothing doing'. Mother's home remedies also included regular doses of castor oil which we all had to take. It came to me between layers of black coffee. It worked – but I still hate black coffee! All water and milk was boiled, food was prepared with fresh ingredients and never kept over more than a few hours, the kitchen was inspected almost every day in the war against dirt, germs and all forms of insects and noxious creatures. Perhaps mother was over careful of her brood, but all seven of her children lived to enjoy a safe and healthy transition from childhood to adult life.

St Kevin's Convent

In 1930 Dad was transferred to the post of assistant Port Health Officer, Madras Port, and we moved out of the hospital quarters to private accommodation in Royapuram. I had started school the previous year, at St Kevin's Convent, Royapuram, but my happy days continued without interruption. In some ways they improved as I gathered school friends, but there were losses, when Viola went away to boarding school and even worse, when Len married and so had less time to play with his baby brother. But school was great for me. I studied in the convent from 1929 to 1933, that is from the infant classes to the 4th Standard. My school reports, carefully preserved by my mother, showed that I usually came second in my class, but there was one girl, Charlotte Rozario, who always seemed to beat me to the top place. In compensation I could claim that additionally I studied the piano and took lessons in elocution. I achieved the Junior Grade with Honours in the Trinity College of Music examinations in pianoforte.

My religion has always been very important to me. I received Holy Communion and was confirmed at the usual early age for Catholic children. I served at mass in Mater Dolorosa's Church and even had the honour of acting as a rather small master of ceremonies at high mass and on ceremonial occasions. One of the tasks entrusted to me was to make up and ensure that the roster of mass servers was maintained. I usually managed to do rather well in Christian doctrine exams and in 1933 I won a certificate of merit in the inter-schools exam and also led the team of boys that won a shield in the oral examination on Christian doctrine.

Perhaps my greatest achievement was in my final year when I was made captain of boys for the whole of St Kevin's. None of this ever prevented me from getting into the usual scraps and whenever I was matched to fight even younger boys, I usually ended up the loser with black eyes and cut lips. But that was only incidental to the bruises and bangs I acquired on the hockey and cricket fields.

My special friends during the years at St Kevin's were my cousins Rudolph Probett, Edgar Platel and Eric Holland and the Harley boys, Clifford, Tony and Robin. We played all the usual games together hockey, cricket, and football. We flew paper kites – my mother was very good at making kites – and strove to entangle the kite strings and sever the other chap's string so that his kite floated away. The kite strings were strengthened with a potent mixture of ground glass and strange ingredients all guaranteed to facilitate your victory in the coming duels. Marbles was a serious game which had an element of gambling – not for money of course, but for marbles and for cigarette cards. My collection of glass marbles was the envy of my friends but I seemed to lose them quite regularly, perhaps I was not as skilful as I believed. I had one huge brass marble which we used to try our strength and skill at putting the shot. I

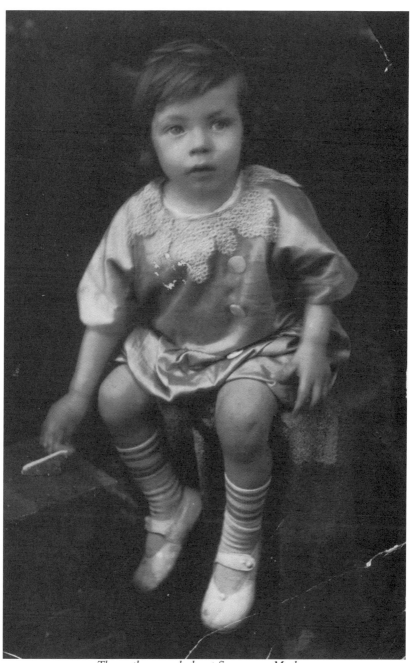

The author aged about five years, Madras

First Communion, aged nine. 1931, Madras

well remember the time that I got in the way of somebody's effort and got the ball straight in my face. It hit my right eye but fortunately it was too big to enter the eye socket, however it did produce quite a lot of superficial damage and bleeding. If there was any compensation I believe that I did rather strut around for weeks with an eyepatch over my right eye – like every respectable pirate.

Except on our home territory, girls, even sisters, did not join in our normal games. My sister Viola and Eric's sister, Phyllis, were the two who seemed to join our quieter games most often. At one time we were asked to set up a team of boys to give the girls stiff opposition at netball. We were instructed to be careful and not play roughly with them but nobody gave the girls a similar warning and we were pushed and barged around and severely beaten by the jubilant girls. A similar exercise at hockey produced a win for the boys but not before we learned, the hard way, that a hockey stick in the hands of an otherwise gentle girl was almost a lethal weapon. These were happy days which changed a bit when we moved on to new schools, Eric and Phyllis Holland to boarding schools in Yercaud, the Harleys to schools nearer their home on the Malabar coast and Rudolph back to his home in Northern India, only Edgar joined me at my new school.

ROYAPURAM

St Mary's European High School

Dad reverted to the Military Department and retired in 1933. The next year I started school in St Mary's European High School, at Armenian Street, George Town, Madras. Life in St Mary's was different. In the first place it was further from home and entailed a journey in the trams or by car. Lunch was brought to us in suitable containers by paid carriers who found one a place in the lunch room and set out the food and almost a table setting for the lucky lads. I no longer had to take music lessons or elocution classes. Yes we had homework – lots of it – but that was normal. Our parents paid for our education and if we failed in the exams, particularly the end of year exams we did not move on to a higher class. The thought of having to spend a further year in the same class with a whole lot of younger boys was a constant source of terror to some of the lads. But I was fairly happy with the regime and continued to do well in my subjects. And one important advantage of being in a bigger school was the chance to have more games and try myself out on the athletics fields. I was never a champion at any of these things but I did love all forms of sport and running and jumping best of all. There was a price to be paid for all this activity. I seemed to have strained my heart and although Dad did not think it was anything very serious, the local heart specialist diagnosed my ailment as angina. Mother took my illness very seriously indeed. I was confined to bed, waited on hand and foot, and naturally missed school for more than three months. This covered the period when I should have been doing my European Middle School exams and also the Junior Cambridge exams. Missing these normally meant that I would not be promoted to the 8th Standard, but Mother saw the Inspector of Schools, showed him my reports for the year, which were all good, and got him to agree that as a very special case I should be allowed to proceed to the higher class. This was agreed subject to proof that I could cope despite the missed period of three whole months. That was all right by me and I continued to show good scholastic progress. But alas, all sport was banned and it was several years before I was allowed to try anything which might tire me out, and by that time I was absolutely useless in comparison to my fellows.

Other than my cousins Edgar and Ralph Platel and classmates, Malcolm Christian, Stan Fernandez, Malcolm Murphy, Dinshaw Antia and Dick Reynolds, I did not have many close friends during my years at St Mary's. This was probably due to my inability to engage in any strenuous activity for most of that time. But of course there were my cousins the Hollands and the Probetts when they came south during the holidays. Rudolph and Anne Probett taught me how to dance. As my heart condition vanished I was encouraged to take up dancing as a mild form of exercise. This absorbed my full attention and with their help I soon became a competent performer and was never at a loss for partners although I did not have a regular girl friend to fill that role.

At the end of the year in the 9th Standard I sat for the European schools High School examination and managed to get a first class and the 7th place overall in the Madras Presidency. My results can be seen on the attached copy certificate. I fear that I was rather pleased to learn that Charlotte Rozario did not manage anything higher than a third class. Revenge at last for all the times she had beaten me while we were at St Kevin's! During my years in St Mary's I collected a few class prizes, particularly in English and religious education and a couple of certificates of merit from the Archbishop of Madras.

Our social life was not one round of parties. Relatives had to be visited on birthdays and at Christmas, each in order of precedence, which meant age. Dad being almost the youngest of his family in Madras was usually left to the end, but at Christmas time he had a great advantage. His birthday was on the

Chapel at St Thomas' Mount, Madras

20th of December and for us it marked the beginning of a season of good cheer. The cakes were all baked by then, the sweets all ready, extra rations of food and drink were readily available and everybody came to us five whole days before Christmas Day. Sadly, Dad seemed to lose many of his gifts of ties and socks before Christmas actually arrived but – that is the fate of fathers with four sons.

The Stevenage clan was always close knit and was large enough to ensure a fair round of 'occasions'. This was an era before radios and television; even gramophones were not often in evidence and good records at a premium. But we made our own fun. There was always somebody around to play the piano or strum on a guitar or banjo, everybody sang – or tried to – reels and dances were practised against the time of the New Year's medical ball or the next popular dance at the Victoria Public Hall; concerts were arranged almost on the spur of the moment and all the regular party games suddenly became popular again. The older generation was kind enough to turn over part of the house for the young folk whose friends were always welcome to join the party. Oh yes, we did have fun and it was all of our own making.

While Madras was the scene for work through most of the year, holiday time hopefully meant a period in Ootacamund or Bangalore. My memories of Ootacamund are very faint, for our holidays there belong to my earliest days. Ooty was cold and for the first time I saw fires in the grates of the bedrooms. We stayed on a hill and I remember going down with the family into the valley below to see the weekly market. Everybody seemed to be there and I can even now picture the crowded scene of milling bodies and riotous colours. My most important memory of Ooty was of the family picnic to Mount Dodabetta which climbed above Ooty to a height of over 8600 feet. Although my sisters should have had the privilege, I, as the youngest, claimed the right to ride on the back of the quiet pony which sedately followed the *syce* up the hill. Yes, Dodabetta was just a hill in a land of real mountains, far to the north. I don't remember much else of the picnic, just the ride on the pony, my first and last one.

Bangalore was my favourite. The weather there was like England in spring and summer throughout the year. Even the rainfall was strictly timetabled to a few hours in the day and to specific months in the year. We had relations in Bangalore, the Lafrenais family and the Bridles, Mary and Barbara Bridle being about my age. But more interesting than any of the others was my cousin, Yvonne Marie (Babs) Texeira, who looked specially attractive to me. And she was a beautiful dancer. Babs and her mother lived with her grandparents, Charlie and Charlotte Lafrenais. Charlotte was Dad's eldest sister. Mother said I should not kiss Babs because I might get some horrible disease which had killed her father. He had contracted leprosy which was a terrible scourge in India. I'm afraid that mother's warnings did nothing to discourage our growing friendship and many kisses were exchanged over the years, adding greatly to the charm of a holiday in Bangalore.

The Stevenages had gathered in Bangalore in force. Johnnie, Dad's brother, taught in St Joseph's College until his death in 1921. Uncle Joe's sons, Eardley, Erwin, Frank and Tony and my brothers Len, Val and Joe all studied at St Joseph's College. Uncle Johnnie owned the Bangalore Pharmacy which on his death passed to the Bridles. Anna Elizabeth Bridle was the youngest of Dad's sisters and on her early death, Bert Bridle married her sister Henrietta Stevenage. Catherine Stevenage lived with her sister Charlotte Lafrenais and from time to time other Stevenages and/or their children appeared and lived there for varying periods. The Lafrenais house, 'Shirley Lodge' on St John's Hill was a comfortable bungalow, large enough to house as many of the family who happened to appear in Bangalore. But at one time Dad's sisters Josephine Platel, Gertrude Carvalho and Catherine Stevenage each owned a house along the same stretch of St John's Church Road. We too bought a place there but after Dad had his first stroke of paralysis (just when he retired) it was decided that it was not going to be a permanent residence for us so it was let and several years later, sold. Bangalore seemed a magnet which drew the Stevenages and even the other branch of the clan had shoots springing up and growing old in its happy climate.

Madras

Loyola College

My parents had decided that I should go to Loyola College, Madras and study mathematics and science there. They were quite prepared to pay all the necessary fees and for all the books that I would need, but it seemed that Lady Luck was on my side and I won a scholarship to Loyola as awarded by the Anglo-Indian Association of Madras. This paid for my fees and left a little over for books and necessaries. It made things easier for my parents, but I was never off a tight budget and I can still remember that my pocket money was the princely sum of 15 Rupees per month all the time I was in Loyola. I went to College, a journey of about eight miles by car or on my bicycle. Lunch was no longer sent from home but bought from the College mess. The facilities at Loyola were wonderful. The Jesuits have always been recognised for their scholastic expertise and for their ability to teach. Our professors were the best in their fields from Europe and from India. We all had to work hard but they managed to draw from us skills which we hardly knew that we possessed. Yes, I did reasonably well and in the intermediate examination of the university (more or less equivalent to the A Levels) and secured distinctions in French, mathematics, physics and chemistry. Dad died on the night before my final exam which was in chemistry, my worst subject. But I went straight from the funeral to the examination hall and to this day I can hardly remember how I did it but I managed to get through the day with some degree of success.

Dad was a wonderful person, always cool and calm and in control of himself. The two most important things in life for him were his family and the practice of his profession. Is it any wonder that he was so loved by all of us? He was a good doctor and I had often heard him say to budding doctors – like my brothers – 'you cannot call yourself a doctor until you have buried your hundredth patient'. No, he was not advocating a trial and error method of medicine but trying to remind them that above all doctors should seek to develop humility and compassion. They were not gods with a power of life or death but just people trying to help to ease suffering and pain and postpone death as long as possible.

World War II broke out in 1939 shortly after I started in college. As I had been born in India I was not liable to be called up in the usual way. I could of course volunteer and many of my friends did just that. Eric Holland left college in the first year to join the RAF. The war seemed far away at first but by 1941 everybody realised that it was getting really serious, even for us so distant from actual danger.

Now arose the question of what I was to do next. Dad had wanted me to follow him and my two elder brothers Valentine and Joseph into the medical profession. I wanted to join the RAF but mother and even my brothers were all against this, so a compromise was agreed – I gave in, went back to college and took economics and politics in the hope that after three years I would qualify with a BA (Hons) and then an MA. This promised to be an easier option than a degree in mathematics or a five year course in the medical college. I did not quite realise just how much I would come to love the subjects I chose as an easy option. Anyway I won a scholarship for a further three years and that was that, it was back to Loyola for me.

A lot of things had changed with the passage of time. Japan entered the war in December 1941 with a sudden attack on the Americans in Pearl Harbour. Shortly before that date, in September 1941, I became an air raid warden and took all the necessary training against the day when the war should come to India's shores. In the eventuality, when Japanese bombers did actually drop about half a dozen bombs on the muddy fields around the Madras airport, I was

The Victoria Public Hall, Madras

enjoying a holiday in Bangalore! We moved from Royapuram to Vepery which was nearer to college and cheaper for rented accommodation. I learned to drive and even passed my driving test which was a joke. Actually I talked my way through the test. I drove into the grounds of the designated police station, picked by my examiner, drove out and around the corner where I stalled the car in the middle of a three-point turn, then I explained to the examiner that I was on my way to the races at Guindy where I had a hot tip in the first race and that Inspector McCarthy had said I would be all right if I mentioned his name and that the examiner should send the driving licence to Bangalore where I was going – by car – the next day. I was not very surprised when the licence arrived in due course – that was India in the time of the British Raj. My driving did not last long because petrol and tyres were both difficult to get and rather than put the car up on its jacks, it was easier to sell the thing and take to my bicycle. But my driving licence is unsullied by any marks of accidents or fines.

On the home front, mother had taken to her bed and become almost a chronic invalid; Valentine and Joseph were both on active service, army doctors; Len worked in the Hindustan Aircraft Factory at Bangalore; Phyllis, who had eloped in 1934 with Ernest Webber, lived with her family in Delhi; Theresa was married in 1937 to Noel Platel who taught me at St Mary's, and for the first time ever had pushed me down from my customary first place in the English exams to an unwelcome second. Even Viola, despite family opposition had married Cecil Dique in 1941. So I was the only chick left in the home nest and continued to be spoiled, but was always careful to keep my growing affection for Babs Texeira from my disapproving mother. Babs remained my only girl friend all through my school and college years and it can well be appreciated just how important holidays in Bangalore became to me.

I continued to do well at my studies and sailed through my term and annual exams. In 1942 I won the gold medal in the inter-collegiate examination in religion. The next year I managed to get the silver medal and then called it a day, not risking any further damage to my reputation in that sphere. I was still largely out of all sporting activity and taking things easy, except for my dancing. I did not have a large circle of college friends. Roche D'Costa, Joseph Lloyd-D'Silva, Ben Wilson, and Cyril Thomas were particular friends in my early years but when Roche and Joseph went to the Medical College my circle was enlarged to include Eddie Ottman, Laurence Gernon, and a whole host of other chaps in that College. They were especially useful when it came to getting tickets for the annual medical ball, but honestly, they remained good friends over the long years that followed. Among my cronies in the later years in college were Mike Matthias, Eric Stracy, Reg Gaughan and Singaram Mudalier.

In 1944 I secured my BA (Hons) with a good 2nd Class (10th place overall in my group of subjects). There were only six Firsts and the fact that I was second in the University in politics no doubt helped push up my ranking.

UNIVERSITY OF MADRAS

Argent, on a mount issuant from the base vert, a tiger passant proper, on a chief sable, a pale or, thereon between two elephants' heads couped of the field, a lotus flower, leaved and slipped on the third.

Motto: "Doctrina vim promovet insitam"

59

Masula boat at Madras, the author as a teenager

Loyola College, Madras

College Chapel

The next year I picked up my MA. The piece of paper that gave me the greatest satisfaction was the reference certificate from Revd Father Basenach, my professor of economics who had the rare privilege among Jesuits of studying under Laski in the London School of Economics.

The war was drawing to a close and my dream of joining the air force had vanished. The civil service seemed to be the best option and so I sat for the federal public service commission examinations. But before the exams I had to fill in a long and detailed questionnaire about my father and my grandfather. I had to say when and where they were born etc etc. Mother could not help much and referred me to Dad's sister, Aunt Gertie. When I cornered her on the subject she professed not to be able to help answer any of the vital questions. I kept on talking and eventually she said that she had a few papers which may or may not be useful. The old dear then produced the original wills of both my grandfather and my great-grandfather. A quick glance showed that they were a veritable mine of information. Both the testators had listed all their living children in their wills and as I read out the names it was almost a roll call because Aunt Gertie's memory came back in full flood and she proceeded to give me dates and places of birth, marriage and death; spouses and children were all named in full and I had almost enough to draw a full family tree just from the data I collected that day. I now had all the facts I needed to answer the official questionnaire and the notes I made and the wills which she presented to me form the basis of much of the family history of the Stevenages in India which I have constructed. From then on I was hooked on genealogy, a subject which still occupies so much of my time.

As part of this civil service examination I had to appear in Delhi for the *viva voce* and this gave me the chance to stay with my sister Phyllis and her family for a short holiday. I took this opportunity to visit the sights of this famous old city, the Red Fort, St James' Church, the Kashmir Gate, the Jami Masjid, Chandni Chowk and the Kutub Minar, where I even climbed the 379 steps to the top to enjoy the magnificent views. Although I did not visit Agra I did have the pleasure of seeing the Taj Mahal looming out of the morning mists as the train steamed through the city.

Then it was back to Madras and the serious business of job-hunting. Perhaps this should mark the opening of another chapter of my saga.

Loyola College

Medals presented to the author by the Archbishop of Madras (see page 58)

64

The author on Graduation Day 1944, Loyola College

LOYOLA COLLEGE
CATHEDRAL P.O.

MADRAS September 8 194 4
PHONE: 6131.

Mr. P.H. Stevenage studied Economic Honours under
me from 1941-1944. He was, in my opinion, the best
student I had for many years, and by best I mean
a student who not only listens & absorbs, but who
questions, sees difficulties, criticises, suggests
and therefore shows intelligence. The rest of my
charges were mostly of the passive sort. I also
found him to be a perfect gentleman throughout,
reliable, industrious and on the best terms with
all his co-students.
I am glad he asks me for a certificate as there
is no risk of my exaggerating the many fine qua-
lities he has shown during his five-years' stay in
our College.

H. Basenach s.j.

Professor of Economics

University of Madras

FACULTY OF ARTS.

The Senate of the *University of Madras* hereby
makes known that __P. H. Stevenage__, who was
admitted to the *Degree of Bachelor of Arts*
(*Honours*) at the *Convocation* held in the year 1944
after having been examined in English and having been
placed in the Second *Class* in *Optional Branch* IV - Economics
——————— of the *Examination in Honours* held
in the year 1944, has now been by us admitted to the
Degree of Master of Arts.

Given under the seal of the University.

Senate House,

February 15, 1945.

A.L. Mudaliar

M.D., LL.D., D.Sc.

Vice - Chancellor.

The Imperial Bank Of India

When I succeeded in getting my degrees from Madras University, I felt on top of the world. But this did not last for very long. A BA (Hons) in Economics and Politics followed by an MA did not seem to automatically produce a good job and an adequate salary. And after all it was only a second class! It seemed that I had to do some more studying and pass some further exams. Because of the war the examinations for the Indian Civil Service had been suspended. I did not fancy the Indian Police, and so I was left with the next best thing – the Indian Audit & Accounts etc Services. This was the entry into the top echelon of the federal services of the government and the 'etc' covered the Indian Railway Accounts Services, the Postal Superintendents Service, and the Transportation (Traffic) and Commercial Departments of the Superior Revenue Establishment of the State Railways. This seemed to suit me and so I put in my application to sit for the entrance examination. Unfortunately the annual total of such applications exceeded 15,000 and my subjects did not seem to fit, I could not offer politics and if I chose to offer rural economics I would have to combine that with a paper on statistics which was quite outside my field. With a sinking heart I decided to offer British and Indian history as two of the required number of additional subjects. Meanwhile, I decided that I had to look in other directions for alternative employment.

One of my friends from Loyola College advised me to try and get into the Imperial Bank of India which was at the time advertising a vacancy in its superior supervisory cadre for a probationary assistant to the agent or branch manager of the bank. As banking, currency and public finance were my 'special subjects' for my degree this looked very promising but my friend warned me that the vacancy was more or less earmarked for a Mr Ipe, the head clerk of the Trivandrum branch of the bank. But he suggested that it was still worth a try. So I slapped in my application and succeeded in getting past the preliminary examination. The next stage was the 'interview' before the local board of the bank. Luck seemed to have stepped into my corner when the telegram calling Ipe for the interview arrived in Trivandrum too late for him to catch the early morning train to Madras. He booked a berth for the next day but alas for him a landslip in the Palghat Gap cut all train communication between Trivandrum and Madras for a further twenty-four hours. He arrived at the bank's head office to learn that I had the job.

But the saga of my first attempt at getting a job was far from over. In my early teens I had strained my heart with excessive sporting activity. After a long spell of rest from all such exercise I had been proclaimed quite fit and it came as a great shock to me when the bank's doctor declared that I was medically unfit for the job which I thought was in the bag. My family doctor was similarly shocked and he strongly suggested that I should appeal against the decision and demand a re-examination by the surgeon general at Madras. Bearing in mind my hopes for alternative employment I complained in the strongest terms and a medical re-examination was arranged. Major Shepherd, the surgeon general of Madras duly examined me and all seemed well. While I was changing in the next room I heard somebody enter Shepherd's office and I was surprised to hear the voice of the bank's doctor who proceeded to inform Shepherd that he had examined me and found me unfit. The inference was clear, that one doctor should support the verdict of another. In a few minutes there was silence next door and I re-entered Shepherd's office. I was more than a little angry at the turn of events but I quietly informed Major Shepherd that I had inadvertently overheard what had transpired and that I fully realised the unwritten code of the medical profession was to support one another. I went on to say that my father and grandfather had also been doctors and that I had two brothers who followed the same profession, one of them holding the same rank as himself, ie a Major in the Indian Medical Service, all of which seemed to entitle me to as much consideration as his recent visitor. Shepherd did not bat an eye and declared roundly that although he had heard his visitor with all due politeness he was not in any way influenced by him and that in his opinion I was quite fit and that that was that. And so it was. But I often wonder what would have happened had I not overheard that vital conversation and strongly pressed my point.

The Imperial Bank graciously accepted that the surgeon general's opinion as to my medical fitness was superior to that of their own doctor. It may be that I was not quite forgiven because I was posted for training to their branch in Trivandrum where Mr Ipe was the head clerk and enjoyed the strong support of the agent. But I did not really worry about such little things, I was on my way in the great world of useful and profitable employment.

I found digs at Trivandrum with Noel and Maisie Isaacs, a couple well-known to my family. Noel worked as a telegraphist and I had had the pleasure of serving at the altar when they had married in our little parish church at Madras. This was the happy and sound base from which, on 1st June 1945, I presented myself at the Imperial Bank of India at Trivandrum to commence my first job.

The work was certainly not taxing and although I was given plenty of time actually working at each task I was quite satisfied with my progress. Then the agent was transferred and a new agent appeared. He was sure that I should move along much faster and this suited me even better. Before nine months had expired I was acting as head clerk and my friend Mr Ipe was moved to another branch.

Everything seemed perfect. Trivandrum was a beautiful town almost hidden from the air by leafy green trees. Although the rain hardly seemed to stop for weeks on end, it was warm and shelter was easily found. Even the mud walls of the compounds wore little thatched hats to preserve them. I joined the

Sri Mulam Club – the Club patronised by the officers of the Native State – and when they presented their annual concert on the occasion of the birthday of HH the Maharaja of Travancore, I was roped in to play the part of 'the saintly and childlike bishop' in a production of 'The Bishop's Candlesticks'. Perhaps it was the skill of the make-up man but the Maharaja looked a bit puzzled when all the cast appeared out of costume on the stage at the end of the show to take their bows. At any rate the dewan, Sir CP Ramaswami Aiyer, introduced me from the stage to the Maharaja, explaining that Mr Stevenage from the Imperial Bank looked very different in evening dress from the bishop in his flowing robes. I think that I owed the unexpected honour of this introduction to the fact that the Maharaja was looking with more than a little warmth at the pretty young lady standing beside me, flushed from our activity at the bottom of the garden, from which we had literally been dragged at the last moment onto the stage. The mother and the sister of the Maharaja had caught his interest and were certainly not amused and so it was left to the urbane Prime Minister to divert all attention from pretty little Kay.

As a 'thank you offering' the dewan arranged a picnic to Kovalam, the beautiful picnic spot just outside Trivandrum, for those members of the cast of our little play presented at the Sri Mulam Club. It did not take too much of an effort on my part to ensure that the offer was finally accepted only by Kay and myself. The day was lovely, the weather, as ever kind; the scene was perfect but alas an assorted crowd of little urchins followed Kay and me wherever we strolled along the beach. We could not even get rid of them to use the only available changing rooms in the local rest house and get into swimming gear. So the day though happy and pleasant must have proved something of a disappointment to our retinue – and also to me!

Trivandrum was a happy little town and I soon found friends. The families of Gallyot, Sweeney, Sawyer, Fertnig, Hoogwerf and Brandenberg spring readily to mind. In particular, I remember a week-end spent at Anjengo with the Brandenbergs. Theirs was a rambling old thatched bungalow set almost on the beach in the middle of a veritable forest of palm trees. I had known their nephew Dirk Brandenburg before his tragic death from haemophilia in Bangalore. Their daughter, Joan, was down on leave from the hospital in Delhi where she was a nurse. We were of about the same age and I had known her when she was a schoolgirl in Madras, the champion sprinter and winner of all her races in the Madras Inter-Schools Championships. We had a lot of friends in common and she was a happy companion on my visit to her home. I well remember my first introduction to 'London'. This was the primitive hole in the floor toilet built on a high raft over the wide backwaters. In the night came the shock of the noises when rats scurried and snakes slithered in pursuit along the lath and linen awnings which stretched below the thatch of the roof and formed what seemed like an insubstantial ceiling to my bedroom. It took me some time to settle down to sleep. Then in the morning came the tall breakfast glass of cold, sweet toddy, freshly tapped from the palm trees in the garden and tasting like champagne. After breakfast we enjoyed a dip in the warm, clear Arabian Sea and a scramble around the ruins of the old Fort that still stood on the beach, to remind visitors that once, long ago, it was the birthplace and home of Elizabeth Draper immortalised in the works of Laurence Sterne.

Maisie Isaacs was a great help when I decided to get an 'engagement ring' made for my girl friend Babs Texeira. We found a dealer in precious stones and he had just the right sort of affordable stone for sale. He was also a jeweller and it was wonderful to watch him set up his little furnace in one corner of the veranda and literally build the ring and set the stone in its gold flower-petal setting. Maisie had suggested the pattern and I was delighted with the result and quickly despatched it hoping that it would be welcomed – it was.

I was still vaguely interested in the Civil Service position for which I had applied earlier, but when I received news that although ranked only 122 out of the thousands of applicants I was in line for the job and should appear for a medical examination at Delhi preparatory to appointment, I decided to ignore the summons. But the powers that be seemed anxious to secure my services and the call to a medical exam was repeated with the suggestion that I would be given the appointment and even a posting to the Madras & Southern Mahratta Railway (which was exactly what I wanted). This time I consulted the new agent of the bank in Trivandrum and he was quite sure that the move would be to my advantage – more money, higher status etc. He suggested that I should write to the headquarters of the bank and explain the position and ask for permission to attend the medical examination at Delhi. He did not think that they would stand in my way and if I passed the medical they would release me from my contract with the bank. So I wrote to the bank and all turned out as he had forecast.

I was enjoying a Christmas break at Cape Comorin, the southernmost tip of India when the call came for me to present myself at the North Western Railway Hospital at Delhi. It was with a slight feeling of trepidation that I dragged myself away from the lovely deep sands of the beach at Cape Comorin where every receding wave seemed to leave three distinctly coloured layers of fresh sand – purple, red and white; and where the sunsets presented an unbelievable riot of colour as a fitting backdrop to the last rocks that marked the end of a wonderfully colourful country. A fifty mile dash by bus to Trivandrum, a train journey of about 24 hours to Madras, a pause for a visit to the Madras Races where I managed to pick the winner of the Governor's Cup on 1st January and then on again by train, a further journey of about 1300 miles taking all of fifty-two hours before I finally arrived in Delhi.

Ernest Webber, the husband of my sister Phyllis, worked in the Government Telegraphs Department at Delhi and he picked me up at the station. A hot bath, a good meal, a comfortable bed and I was ready for my second encounter with the dreaded doctors. This time there was no hesitation, I was pronounced A1 fit. Then I had to dash back all the way to Trivandrum via Madras.

Getting a berth on the Grand Trunk Express from Delhi to Madras was always a bit of a problem. On a previous visit to Phyllis I had to share the floor of a compartment with a huge Alsatian dog which stretched out in front of the door to the toilet and growled alarmingly at everyone attempting to pass that threshold. I was determined that I should approach the problem differently this time. I got my name onto the list of applications for a berth and refusing to be daunted by the discouraging remarks of the staff, set about my new plan. I had learned after my last visit that the staff of the reservation office at Delhi were working a racket of their own. Mr Shah, the chap in charge of the reservation list was the king-pin in this game and nobody got a reservation unless he was suitably rewarded. I found Mr Shah, who was armed with a whole file of lists, and put my modest request to him. 'Not a hope, the train is booked solid for weeks'. I moved to stage two of my plan. I explained that I had come to Delhi for a medical exam at the hospital of the headquarters of his own railway and that as I had passed I expected to be posted as Assistant Traffic Superintendent to his railway (this latter statement was not exactly true) and that I would certainly remember the assistance, if any, he gave me in my search for a humble berth on the Grand Trunk. Success! Mr Shah turned over to a new section of his file and I was offered a choice of any berth I wanted, upper or lower, in any of half a dozen compartments. I had a very comfortable journey back to Trivandrum and in due course was notified of my appointment to the position of apprentice Assistant Transportation Superintendent (Traffic) on the Madras & Southern Mahratta Railway. As predicted by the agent, the bank accepted my resignation, refunded my security deposit and wished me luck with my new career.

Kovalam Beach

Trivandrum, 1945

The Madras and Southern Mahratta Railways Board Headquarters

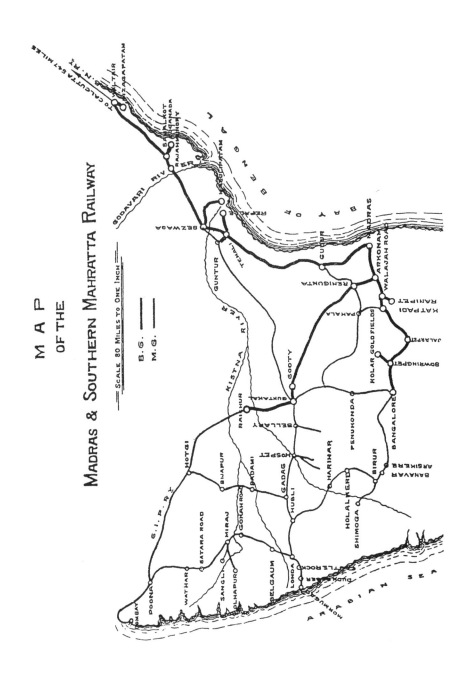

MAP
OF THE
MADRAS & SOUTHERN MAHRATTA RAILWAY

SCALE. 80 MILES TO ONE INCH

B.G.
M.G.

76

The Madras & Southern Mahratta Railway [M&SM]

Early on the morning of 11th March 1946 I appeared at the headquarters of the Madras & Southern Mahratta Railway in Madras and asked to see the General Manager, Mr R de K Maynard. I was expected and when I presented my copy of the Government of India Railways Board's letter of appointment I was quickly ushered into his office. He was a charming gentleman who quickly made me welcome and put me at my ease. He explained that I would have to take a full period of training as a probationer and pass through all the stages of working on the railway before I could take up my appointment as an Assistant Transportation Superintendent (Traffic). As my mother was in a poor state of health I requested to be posted as near to Madras as possible at least in the first stages of my training. He said that that could be arranged if I explained the position to Mr Sarkies, the Deputy Chief of Operations (Staff).

And so I was passed down the line to Mr Sarkies who was seated at an imposing desk in another grand office. He seemed to be a nice sort of chap who for some reason seemed to be engaged in an inspection of the pens and pencils on the elaborate pen rack in front of him. He picked them up one by one and frowned or smiled at them before replacing them on the rack. I thought that this was mainly for my amusement and he suddenly looked up to find me smothering a laugh which he obviously interpreted as being at his expense. Yes, he was very pleasant but I found that I was posted to the Hubli District, as far away from Madras as possible and when I got there Mr Marwar the District Traffic Superintendent decided that I should commence my training at Belgaum, almost as far north of Madras as one could get without leaving the boundaries of the M&SM railway. The first lesson I was to learn was that Chief Officers were not to be laughed at – even if they behaved very oddly.

Training In Railway Accounts

When I arrived at Hubli I was introduced to the other Traffic Officers who happened to be in the headquarters that day and on raising the question of where I should stay in Belgaum, I was referred to Mr Angelo, the Assistant Transportation Superintendent (Traffic). He suggested that I would have no trouble on that score and that on arrival at Belgaum I should look up a Mr Delamotte, the Signals Inspector, who would be sure to help me to find suitable digs. But Delamotte was out 'somewhere on the line' when I reached Belgaum and his mother did not seem to be any great help at first. But then she caught on to my name and said that her mother had been a Stevenage. The whole atmosphere changed and she soon had me fixed up in a cottage rented out by Mr and Mrs Giels who also agreed to provide me with full board for the period of my stay in Belgaum. Years later I traced the connection between the Delamotte family and the Stevenages – we were very distant cousins. But hurrah for the family connection!

The Giels had two other guest boarders; Henry Gomez, a Deputy Superintendent of Excise, and Helen Smith his girl friend. They also had two daughters, Barbara and Isabel and a young son, Edward. The house was always filled with young people, friends of the family and young officers from the Mahratta Light Infantry which had its HQ at Belgaum. I had fallen on my feet and could not have wished for a happier environment for the first stage of my railway training.

Of course I was there to learn all about the commercial side of railway working; the sale of tickets from the booking office; the hire of wagons and the conveyance of parcels and small consignments of goods, all arranged in the Goods and Parcels Offices. I even had to stand by for the best part of a day and watch the ticket collectors gather in and account for used passenger tickets. I'm afraid that I did not worry too much about the mechanics of the railways commercial activity. Fresh from the rigorous discipline of banking the railway accounting systems seemed simple but over elaborate. I quickly mastered that part of the work and managed to slip away from the office whenever I wanted. What proved to be a real eye-opener was the extent of corruption that went on between the chief Goods Clerk and the Station Master who demanded, and received, an additional personal tariff from every trader before they would 'find' wagons to accommodate the goods offered for carriage. These two gentlemen were Tamilians whereas the rest of the staff were Marathi speakers. All their negotiations were carried on in Tamil and nobody else seemed to understand the true state of affairs. That is – except for me! My Tamil has always been quite good and although I did not give any indication that I was following their discussions, I learned exactly how the system worked. This was a lesson which was to prove invaluable when, in due course, I had to control staff and undertake anti-corruption enquiries on my own district. The Station Master seemed to have been given the idea that he should dictate the pace of my training and that I should be more under his control. One morning when I was having a late lunch in the Refreshment Rooms he looked in to remind me that I should be in the booking office. I quickly commenced an elaborate discussion of the menu with the waiter, speaking in Tamil, his native tongue. The Station Master became very agitated as he realised that I must be aware of all his little games in the goods shed. He exclaimed 'I didn't know that you could speak Tamil, Sir'. I do not suppose that my answer helped when I replied ' Oh yes, and I understand it even better than I can speak it'. No more problems from that quarter.

These were happy days for me, with parties, party games and dancing most evenings. Some mornings, we played cricket in the garden and when it rained everybody changed into swimming costumes and continued the match. Then we loaded the girls onto the crossbars of our cycles and rode through the market singing at the tops of our voices – something about the rain never falling on the just! We arranged picnics and went to Khanpur, an ideal spot a few

Belgaum, 1946. Main-line train crossing the bridge

With friends at Belgaum, 1946

miles out of town where a river flowed under a railway bridge. George Delamotte provided his Railway Inspector's saloon for our use and a wonderful time was had by all. Among our army friends was the Station Staff Officer, Captain Ward; Lieutenant O'Connor, who was a little in love with Barbara Giels; and several others, whose names have vanished in the mists of time. Every now and then when the Customs seized large quantities of wine being smuggled out of Goa and into India, Henry Gomez's clerk used to bid for a few bottles when they came up for auction. Needless to say his bids were always successful and wine flowed at dinner that evening.

But all good things had to come to an end and after a month I was ordered to report back to Hubli to see the District Traffic Superintendent. If he felt I had successfully passed the first stage of my railway training I was instructed to report to the Audit Office in Madras. I left Belgaum for Hubli and went to see Mr Marwar but he did not seem very interested in me or my report of progress. We chatted for a bit and I was told to carry on. So I followed my orders and went down to Bangalore to see my girlfriend, Babs, at the week-end before going on to Madras. Marwar tried to say that I had not reported to him and had taken unauthorised leave before appearing at the audit office. But I had my piece of paper with my orders and the correct dates. As I had met some of the other railway officers in Hubli when I reported there he found himself without any support for his complaint. I have always got on well with auditors and Menon and Batliwallah, the two Senior Auditors, confirmed my response to Marwar's complaint and so he had to drop the subject. But he did not forget me and much later, when he was promoted to Deputy Chief Operations Superintendent (Staff) he tried to raise his complaint once more but somebody must have told him not to make a fool of himself and that was the end of my first brush with petty authority on the railways.

Each stage of my training programme was planned to last either a fortnight or a month and the first stage was a month. The Audit Office was located in the main building of the headquarters in Madras. This meant that I could live at home which was a great relief to me and to my mother whose health seemed to improve because I was near.

The work there was simple but interesting. I had to spend time with the cashiers who checked the contents of the travelling cash-chests into which all stations loaded the daily cash takings and accounting returns. The movement of these chests was carefully planned and security was always watertight. Next, I had to see the accounts submitted by the stations being checked agreed with the cash collections and aggregated monthly and annually to build up into the total accounts of the railway. A quick peek into the workings of the independent government auditors and I was ready to move on again.

It was decided that I should be attached to the travelling Inspector of Accounts stationed at Jalarpet to get practical auditing experience of the accounts prepared and submitted by stations as against the various basic records kept at source. The auditor concerned turned out to be my cousin Edward Platel, so the arrangement proved a very happy one. I lived in the Rest Rooms at Jalarpet, slipped away to Bangalore every week-end to see Babs, and delighted Edward with my willingness and ability to balance accounts quickly and take over a full share of his workload during each and every audit for the month I was attached to him.

It was while I was on this stage of my training that I had my first ride on the footplate of an engine. This was certainly not part of my programme but happened quite accidentally when the first train going towards Bangalore one Friday evening was delayed and its path was taken by a 'light engine' ie an engine operating without a load of any sort. The driver, Gerry Tanner, was a nice chap who had recently suffered a distressing experience when an Indian woman committed suicide by throwing herself on the rails in front of the fast passenger train he was driving. He said that he would never forget the way she clutched the rail and looked up and even smiled at the approaching engine. She had chosen her spot well and he had no hope of stopping his train in time to save her life. He had been taken off his regular shift for a few weeks and rested on light traffic runs but he certainly did not slow down and I was really scared as I held on to the iron railing in the engine cab and saw the train rush at speed into every curve, apparently without anybody being in a position to guide it safely around the track. But all was well and we arrived in Bangalore safely and indeed, early. Gerry Tanner recovered and much later I met him again when he was the Assistant (Motive Power) Controller at Guntakal.

Training In Railway Operating

The next stage of my programme was designed to teach me all about the running of trains and that meant firstly a few weeks in the Railway School in Madras. For this stage of training I was joined by Robert Amrithraj who had been posted at the same time as me to the Madras and Southern Mahratta railway.

The railway school in Madras was really fascinating. We joined a class of about twenty and were taught how the train service was controlled, firstly by the pointsmen who shifted the points and guided the train from one track to another, then by the signalmen and station masters who directed the movement of the train by changing the signals which were the authority for a train driver to move his charge along the tracks within the limited areas of a station yard and the longer stretches between stations. The whole system was a mass of controls, electrical, mechanical, vocal and written. Everything was done to make sure that at no time could two trains enter the same stretch of track. An 'absolute block system' was the rule we worked to.

81

We were introduced to the 'bible' of operating rules; we were allowed to play with the model sets of track, signalling and trains in the long instruction hall. It was not really a game because at every step we were under the watchful eyes of instructors who made sure that we knew all the rules and the importance of each seemingly trivial instruction. We literally had to operate the model set up, control the points, the signals and the trains. We were taken out into the railway yards, signal boxes and stations and watched the staff at their daily work, then back to the school where we became the staff of the model railway system, operating all its machines, systems and controls.

No, we were never allowed to drive a real engine but had to be content with learning the hard job of coupling wagons by hand and all the duties and responsibilities of the various grades of guards who 'worked' the different classes of trains. Of course we had to pass the St John Ambulance training to enable us to give qualified First Aid in emergencies. It was a serious business and everybody had to pass the final examinations that qualified them as signallers, station masters or guards. They had only to pass the one examination appropriate to their grades, we had to pass all the grades and the instructors really tested us out with every conceivable problem and difficult set of circumstances they could contrive. It became a real battle of wits played under the keen eye of the chief instructor and the overall majesty of the book of rules. I had a wonderful time in the railway school and I like to think that I learned a lot about railways and their operations.

When I finished at the railway school I was put to work on the real thing. First I had to work as a guard and for this part of my training I was posted to the Guntakal district which covered almost the whole of the metre gauge sections of the Madras and Southern Mahratta railway.

I reported to the District Transportation Superintendent (Traffic) at Guntakal, was introduced all round and then turned over to the Station Superintendent at the headquarters station of Guntakal. He arranged for me to stay in the Retiring Rooms over the station and the Refreshment Rooms below provided me with very good food on demand for the length of my stay there.

I told the Station Superintendent that unlike some of the other probationers I wanted to actually work the trains and undertake all the duties and responsibilities of a guard. He was delighted and I soon found myself in charge of long distance goods trains, stopping goods trains that loaded and unloaded at all stations on a route, local passenger trains, and even fast mail trains. I slipped into the various services as gaps occurred due to sickness or other emergencies. I did not wear a uniform but I did get to blow a whistle and wave a flag whenever necessary. I also came very near to death on one occasion.

The trains in India had doors which opened inwards and broad footboards. Everybody quickly learned to swing on or off moving trains without any real risk to life or limb and I mastered this art at a very early stage of my training and happily jumped on or off trains when they were half-way out of the railway platforms.

One day, when I was in charge of a road goods train, the driver forgot that he had a water tank wagon to be detached just one station before his journey ended. We steamed happily through until he noticed that the station master and all his staff, in full uniform, were standing on the platform to greet his train – they had discovered that a probationary officer was acting as the guard. He rapidly applied the brakes and started to back onto the platform and I stepped off the train to speak to the station master. But I had forgotten that when a train is backing one should face the rear of the train when jumping off. Down I tumbled into the dust where I tripped over and landed on the track with my neck on a very cold rail. I can still see the wheel of the wagon next to my brakevan as it rolled towards me. I kicked out desperately and pushed sideways as hard as I could. Because the platform was a low 'continental' type I managed to roll myself off the track and onto the platform. Everyone rushed forwards but feeling ashamed of my incompetence I waved them away and proceeded to un-couple the water tank and guide it into its siding. When the train pulled away I collapsed onto the seat in my brake-van, my hands shaking so much that I could hardly hold a match to the cigarette I needed to steady my nerves.

That was my only adventure when working as a guard and when my period of training was over I went back to Madras to find that my next posting was to a signal box at Tenali on the Bezwada district.

The district operating superintendent at Bezwada was a Mr Hooper, a colourless sort of person who left little impression on anybody. He was notable only for a petty stubbornness which became evident when he thought that his authority was being challenged. The other officers at Bezwada included Jerry Baldrey, the assistant personnel officer and his brother Cyril, the chief traffic controller. Their sister Mabel was the wife of my cousin Edward Platel and so once more I landed amongst friends.

Tenali was an important station, just south of Bezwada on the line to Madras. The north signal cabin controlled the main line traffic heading for Bezwada and also the branch line trains to and from Guntur. The station master asked me whether I would like to have the regular signalman with me when I was left 'in charge' of the cabin but I felt quite capable of controlling the work and suggested that the regular incumbent would enjoy a spell of leave. So there I was in charge of an important signal box on the east coast main line with only an old but very capable pointsman to help me handle the levers, and keep the place tidy. Signal levers have highly individual characteristics and to 'pull off' a distant signal entailed a rather special jerk at the end of a strong haul. I quickly mastered these arts and learned the train services that fell into my daily shifts. The regular signalman departed happily on his unexpected spell of leave and I settled into his rostered duties.

My month in the signal box was uneventful except for the occasion when the station – and of course the signal boxes – were inspected by the chief government inspector of railways in the course of his annual tour of the district. The station master again offered to bring back the regular signalman for this inspection but I indignantly refused. Actually the chief inspector was quite charming and did not ask me any tricky questions although he watched me closely as I handled the token authority machines, exchanged codes with the main station and my opposite number in the signal box ahead and lowered and locked the various signals as necessary. After the day's work I was delighted to receive an invitation from him to drinks in his saloon where the district superintendent and the escorting officers had also assembled. The next day I cheerfully waved him away as he departed on the first train heading north to Bezwada.

Training In Railway Engineering And Commercial Departments

When this part of my training was complete I was returned to the headquarters at Madras where I again joined up with Amrithraj for a spell in the chief civil engineers drawing office and in the claims office of the chief commercial manager. We were not required to do more than learn the principles and procedures in these offices and the time passed pleasantly. I must admit that I was not particularly impressed to learn that every claim had to be denied as a first response and followed by a process of bargaining when the reports came to hand from the station masters and the traffic inspectors concerned. But that was the accepted way of dealing with claims and I now knew what was expected of me when in due course I had to prepare reports on damages and to decide on claims made against the administration.

Train Control

My programme of training took me back to Bezwada again and this time I was to be introduced into the world of train controlling. I came to love this part of the railway work far more than any other.

The control office was equipped with a series of charts showing graphs of the scheduled trains running over the whole district during a twenty-four hour period. Seated opposite these diagrams were a group of section controllers whose duty was to create clear records of the actual performance of the train service as reports of passing trains came in from stations and signal boxes. The controllers decided on all variations to the programmed service made necessary by late running and ensured that delays were minimised. It should be remembered that we operated a single line 'absolute block system' and that only one train could occupy any stretch of the track at any particular time. An error of judgement by a controller could result in long delays to important trains which were held at stations waiting for the incoming service to cross or for the train ahead to clear the section. The controller had to estimate the speed and timing of all trains on his section, take into account the weather and any special problems on the track or with the engines and rolling stock. It was the game we had played in the Railway Training School but this time we had additional problems created by difficult passengers, inefficient staff and defective engines or rolling stock. The chief controller and his deputies prowled around the control room constantly watching everything that happened and intervening whenever necessary. Each control desk was equipped with a telephone keyboard connecting the section controller to every station and signal box on his area. Additionally there were overriding systems of telephones for the chief and his deputies.

Passenger traffic control was the easier part of the job. The real problems arose when trying to control freight traffic. A careful study of the track distances, gradients and available engine and brake controlling power available resulted in the advance creation of a maximum series of 'paths' for trains over the sections. Passenger trains had first call on the available number of paths and the rest were there to be taken up by the freight trains as and when required. The real problem was that the flow of freight traffic was erratic, seasonal and dependent on the state of trade and the economy in general. Goods wagons were demanded by traders in advance of their needs and there was a difficult system of official priorities given to the various types of goods. We were just emerging from World War II and everything was in short supply – engines, brake-vans, wagons, and commodities of all kinds. Food had the first priority, then came coal, oil, minerals, machinery and manufactures in that order. The job of creating some sort of operating plan out of the varying daily demands and available facilities fell to the freight controllers, operating as a separate section within the control office. They had the hardest job of all and one that required not only a wide knowledge of the economy of the district but also firmness and tact when dealing with traders, commercial staff and even with their train-operating colleagues. I loved the art of planning in advance the movement of railway stock to meet demand for these facilities at the key points on the system and the daily scramble to match supply and demand. I was not allowed to take over the duties of a section controller or a freight controller on a regular basis but I did have the chair for short periods and even functioned as a deputy controller and as the chief controller, which was considered a much safer option for a trainee. Although the responsibility was greater, the scope for error was considerably reduced because of the quality of the staff engaged at the lower levels.

In the course of my control office training I was sent out into the yards for brief spells to see how incoming freight trains were broken up and reassembled in formations suitable for onward despatch to stations and junctions en route to their destinations. Wagons which were not fully loaded to destination points had to be sorted and repacked. Where broad gauge and metre gauge services met – as they did at Bezwada – whole wagon loads had to be transhipped from one type of wagon to the other. The sorting and transhipment sheds were always a hive of activity where a knowledge of railway geography was an essential requirement. Every train arriving in or leaving the station yards was checked by the busy number-takers who recorded not only the number of each wagon but its destination, load and load weight. There too the fussy shunting engines and shunters ruled, pushing and pulling wagons from place to place and from line to line.

Early every morning, before the rest of the world was awake, the clerks in the control office compiled and reported to the railway operations headquarters in Madras the timekeeping of all trains on the district, the numbers of trains and wagons received into the district, the numbers of wagons loaded and despatched, the number of outstanding demands for wagons and the availability of engines and brakevans. Of course any special occurrences, accidents, floods, landslips etc all received special mention. The assistant traffic superintendent, movements, and the chief controller reviewed all this data and in due course made a personal report to the chief operations manager or his assistant on the progress of the day and the prospects for the future. The chief operations manager had to balance the demands for rolling stock and power over the whole of the railway, and in particular, the interchange of facilities at points where the different railway systems met. At Bezwada the Madras & Southern Mahratta railway met the Nizam of Hyderabad's railway and they had their own engines, wagons, etc. Charges were levied for the use of one system's stock by the other railway company.

While I was in the control office at Bezwada I was surprised one morning by the arrival of a bullock-cart from which a young man was carried unconscious, and laid on the ground outside the office. He had been bitten by a cobra. Distraught relatives dashed into the office and demanded that a message be passed over the control telephone line to 'Pambu Narasiah' one of our station masters down the line. In a few minutes he answered the phone and asked only two questions. When had the man been bitten, and was he conscious or unconscious? There was a short pause and he then assured the anxious people that they were not to worry and that the lad would live. About twenty minutes later the victim of the snake bite, which often proved to be fatal, got up, asked for a drink of water, climbed back into the cart and set off for home. This experience would have been absolutely astonishing had I not heard about 'Pambu Narasiah' and his strange powers from a friend many years earlier. 'Pambu' in Tamil means snake and Narasiah was a railway employee who had the 'power' to cure snakebite from a distance, as I had indeed witnessed. He had refused promotion many times asking only to remain on the main line where he could be reached by the quick railway telephone system.

The story that I heard from my friend Cecil Rodriques, a railway auditor, was that on one occasion when he was returning from the station to the railway rest-house which he occupied while auditing the station's accounts, he was struck on the leg by a king cobra, one whose bite was fatal in most cases. Cecil was a calm, matter-of-fact sort of person. He hurried into the rest-house, applied iodine to the bite and settled down to write his Will! His bearer, meanwhile dashed to the station, alerted the staff there and asked for a message to passed to Narasiah who was the station master of the next station down the line. His response was prompt and reassuring. 'Tell the Sahib that all will be well and that I shall come there myself and prove my powers to him'. By chance there was a train at his station waiting to move off in the right direction and within a quarter of an hour Narasiah had appeared at the rest-house. Meanwhile, the usual crowd of curious onlookers had gathered around. Narasiah asked for a saucer of milk which was quickly provided. He placed this on the ground and squatted a few feet in front of the milk. He waved the crowd back and they formed a circle around him as he began to chant some mantras which were quite incomprehensible to Cecil who was lying on a camp bed on the veranda. In a few minutes there was a rustle and the crowd quickly parted as a king cobra slid into the circle and reared itself up in front of the saucer of milk. It struck three times at the milk discharging its venom and then the crowd moved forward prepared to strike out at what was now a harmless snake. Narasiah would have none of that. 'Let it go in peace, it has made amends' he said. Cecil swore that as the snake struck at the milk he felt the poison drain from his leg and that as it vanished into the bushes he was able to get up and thank Narasiah and withdraw into the rest-house to recover from what had been an unnerving experience. No, I have no explanations to offer. Many strange things happen in India. This is a true tale of one such strange happening.

Training: Station Working

The next stage of my training gave me the opportunity to work as assistant station master of the joint Madras & Southern Mahratta railway and the Nizam's railways station at Bezwada. I took up the full duties of the post and held charge for early, late and night turns of duty, relieving the regular ASM to enjoy a well-earned month's leave. It was a very exciting time both for my work and for India which was hurrying towards Independence from Britain.

It was quite clear to me that a change in government would mean a change in my service conditions and prospects of promotion. I felt that in these difficult and changing conditions it would be only right and proper to offer to release Babs from our unofficial engagement. She said, 'Thank you, but no. We will face the future together even though we may have to leave India and settle somewhere else.' That was what I had hoped she would say and so our plans to get married as soon as possible remained unaltered.

On the work front one turn of night duty – my first, I think – will always remain clear in my mind. I was due to take over at 8 pm but a few moments before that the man I was to relieve dashed into the refreshment room, where I was having an after-dinner coffee, and pleaded for me to come and help as a difficult situation had arisen on the platform. The train from Calcutta to Madras was ready to depart but two members of the Central Legislative Assembly, one a Hindu and the other a Muslim, had come to blows arguing about who had the right to a sleeping berth in a particular First Class compartment. Well, I got in between them and joked a bit but made them see that they were holding themselves and their high office open to ridicule. I managed to find a vacant berth in another compartment and settled them down and waved the train away with a sigh of relief. But the night had only just begun.

A little after 9 pm a freight train from the Nizam's railway approached the station and the north signal box keeper asked me to allocate a line in the crowded yard for its reception. I consulted the line occupation chart I had received from the outgoing ASM and allocated a line, but something made me suspicious and so I sent my pointsman ducking under the intervening lines of wagons to check that the line allocated was indeed clear of all traffic. He was back in less than a couple of seconds. 'The line is blocked at the south end Sahib by wagons placed there without any record.' I dashed to my control panel and reversed the signals that the north box signal man was in the process of lowering. Then out into the yard to verify a truly clear line and back to yell a revised order to the signal box. What I later discovered was that just recently a regular ASM had been placed under suspension because he had caused a technical 'averted collision' by admitting an incoming train onto an occupied line in the yard. To bolster his defence that the rule was impractical, a plan had been hatched between him and the signals staff to get me to commit a similar offence which could then be quoted by him. But hard luck, I had managed to escape the trap – but only just.

Settled back in my office the night seemed to be running a calm course when at about 2 am my pointsman asked for authority to lower the signals for a passenger train to depart from the bay track. I told him to sound the departure bell and then lower the signal and strolled out to see the train leave. There was a sudden scream and the train jerked to a stop as the communication cord was pulled. A sick old beggar had been sleeping on the track under the last carriage of the train. He did not appear to have heard the departure bell and the train ran over him cutting him almost in half. All we could do was rope off the area, disconnect the last coach, transfer the passengers inside to the rest of the train and get it on its way. The railway police who had been summoned made the usual belated appearance and I was thankful to hand over control of the situation to them.

Dawn was breaking when another train came in from the Nizam's line. The *syce* [groom] in charge of a horse-box taking the Nizam's racehorses to a race meeting in Madras felt in need of some more fresh air and so he threw open the large half-top doors of the horse-box, which, being oversized for our system, knocked over a signal post as it entered the station area. The train examiners and the signals staff were summoned to inspect and make emergency repairs. Statements were taken and reports compiled. Only one hour to go and I began to relax but the horrors of that memorable night were not over as yet.

The mail train from Madras to Calcutta came in and stopped on the platform for the engine crew change as planned. The outgoing staff refused to take over the job because the fires on the engine had banked solid and would require half an hour of hard raking before the train could proceed. The incoming crew had fallen down on their job. So I was summoned to smooth tempers, get the fires raked out thoroughly and then the train was ready to depart. Walking back to my office I noticed a crowd of people standing on the platform and looking hard at a particular First Class carriage. The laughter drew me to join them and to my horror I found that two European men and two women, continentals who were unfamiliar with our trains, had stripped down to the very minimum of underwear and were just rising out of their sleeping berths and moving around the compartment. They did not realise that only the wire-mesh shutters had been lowered and that whereas they could not see outside everybody on the platform was enjoying the nudist show within. I felt something of a spoilsport when I banged on the door and told the passengers to get dressed quickly and to shut the compartment windows properly. My turn of duty had come to an end but I still had to write up the official diary of the night's horrors and attend the inquest into the fatality. It was lunch time when I finished and was free to have a meal. Then I was due back on duty at 4 pm. The joint station master afterwards told me that he had kept himself informed of everything as it happened that night and never in all his years of experience had such a succession of accidents occurred. He said that it might be some consolation to me to know that he felt confident that I could not only cope with what had happened but that I should never be scared of any future nightmare of a duty turn even if I lived to be a hundred. I am not sure that I felt better for his confidence in me.

In June 1947 it was announced that India would become independent on 15 August and as that date approached, the troubles that some of us had expected began. Hindus massacred Muslims and in turn were massacred by their Muslim neighbours who had lived peacefully beside them for so many years. Lord Mountbatten had set a timetable for independence and nothing was going to delay that. Lines were drawn to separate the future state of Pakistan from what was left – India. Nobody wanted to pause and make sure that these boundaries were viable, ethnically correct or even just. The programme rolled on and so did the killings.

In Bezwada I witnessed a small part of the madness that had taken over a hitherto peaceful country. The Grand Trunk Express was perhaps the most important train in India. It ran from Delhi to Madras, taking about fifty-two hours to travel some 1300 miles. Rumours began to spread that on many occasions en route it was being attacked and the passengers slaughtered. At Bezwada, where the train moved from Muslim Hyderabad State into India, I found proof of this. On several occasions when it arrived the only people left alive on the train were Europeans or Indian Christians. As the train had passed through Hindu areas the Muslims were killed and as it progressed into Muslim areas the Hindu passengers suffered the same fate. The terrified remnants of what had been fully loaded trains were taken off at Bezwada and treated to hot meals and drinks of tea or coffee in the Refreshment Rooms. The train itself was pushed into the traffic yard and the sweepers were put in to wash away the blood which caked the floors of the compartments, inches deep. This happened on several occasions when I was the assistant station master on duty at Bezwada.

Babs and I decided that it would be better for us to marry while India still remained British and I still had my good job. July 21 was a suitable date and I managed to arrange ten days leave to enable me to get down to Bangalore, marry and have a very short honeymoon. Knowing that my mother would not be happy with my decision, I did not tell her in advance and similarly kept the news from the rest of the family. The date chosen was after I was due to finish my next period of training – as a station master. Then I would have to return from my short honeymoon and pick up the duties of a district traffic inspector which would keep me travelling around the district constantly for a month. I could then dash down to Bangalore and bring Babs back with me to Bezwada. A tight programme with many arrangements to be made as quietly as possible.

But it all worked out well and I spent my month as the station master at Ellore in something of a daze. I already knew the routine of the job and nothing of any great interest happened.

Then came the great day and I was off to Bangalore arriving there early on the morning of July 21 and getting to the church well on time. The bride was as lovely as ever and my best man, Melville Gaughan handled all the usual chores with his customary efficiency and goodwill. My only sorrow was that none of my immediate family was present.

My honeymoon passed like a dream and, before I knew it, I was back in the office at Bezwada being briefed by Jerry Baldrey before taking up my duties as the traffic inspector at Rajahmundry. He asked me what I had done on my leave and could not believe it when I replied, 'I got married'. The establishment code of the railways did not require me to notify the authorities or request permission from my superiors before marrying. It was my affair and I had kept it so. Jerry only really began to believe me when I presented him with a piece of the wedding cake!

As a traffic inspector I had to oversee the working of the stations and the operation of the services on a section of the district allocated to my control. It

Bangalore Cantonment Station today

was a mixture of staff supervision, inspection of working conditions, passenger and freight working, commercial duties, enquiries into accidents, complaints from the public, assessment of damages to goods and parcels in our care and in fact every bit of the railway work that fell above the scope and authority of a station master but below that of the district superintendent and his assistants.

While I was acting as the traffic inspector I was instructed to ensure that all the staff on my area took an oath of allegiance to the new government of India on August 15. I was rather amused at this because I was not asked to take any such oath myself and would not have consented to do so. But I visited all the stations and depots on my section, duly administered the prescribed oath of allegiance and prepared and forwarded a complete list of the 'loyal' staff to the district headquarters. Much to my surprise, when I reached Cocanada Port, I was greeted by my old friend the station master from Belgaum who had been transferred there since we had last met. He looked very worried indeed until I reassured him as to the reason for my visit and casually mentioned that I would shortly be moving on from the Rajamundry district back to the district head-quarters at Bezwada. He did not ask me if I could speak Telegu as fluently as I spoke Tamil!

Training: Miscellaneous Departments

Time seemed to drag a bit until the weekend when I was free to dash down to Bangalore, pick up Babs and, armed with a new free railway pass in her new name, whisk her off to Bezwada. The stages of training that followed seemed to be longer but certainly not as exciting as those which had gone before. I had to spend quite a lot of time in the district office learning the esoteric arts of staff management and stores management. Then the engineers could not be lightly passed over. There were civil engineers, mechanical engineers, electrical engineers and signal engineers and they all had something important to teach me because all these disciplines came together to run a railway. It was indeed fortunate that Babs was installed in the Rest Rooms with me and that made it easier for me to settle down to learning everything that was pushed at me. We also began to make friends with some of the other inhabitants of Bezwada. Hooper and his wife held themselves aloof and so we ignored them. The Baldreys, Pansey, the joint station master and Selvey, the locomotive foreman all went out of their way to be friendly and entertain us particularly as there was now a new young bride to grace the railway colony.

One night when I got back to the Rest Rooms I found an order waiting for me from Hooper. I was instructed to vacate the room and make it available for an important political visitor to the town. It was then after midnight and I quickly took stock of the position. There was another small rest room available and I arranged to move all the effects of another railway officer from his large room into the small one. He was out on line but I caught him when he arrived early the next day and he agreed that I had done the only sensible thing. The joint station master and Jerry Baldrey also concurred. Only Hooper climbed on his high horse and called me into his office for a ticking off. He had bitten off more than he could chew. I agreed that he was entitled to make any order that he saw fit but pointed out that it was ineffective until it reached me. I had only returned to the Rest Rooms after midnight but if he had looked over the garden wall of his quarters he would have seen Babs and me having dinner, and later coffee and drinks in the garden with Jerry Baldrey, his staff officer who lived just next door to him. I went on to point out that the other officer who was living in the Rest Rooms had an official bungalow allocated to him which he had not occupied as yet and which was lying empty and so the railway was losing revenue on it. He had not objected or been put to any inconvenience by my actions and I was being forced to the unhappy conclusion that he, Mr Hooper, was for some unknown reason trying to make life uncomfortable for me and my wife. How would he like me to take my complaint to the chief? That was that. Hooper would never be a friend but he was clearly caught in an awkward position. Nothing more was said but I quickly made arrangements for Babs and myself to stay with the Selvey family and Selvey was not answerable to Hooper for anything. In fact as I had to move on to a spell of training in the locomotive sheds and the motive power department, it was a very convenient arrangement.

My time in Bezwada had come to an end and I had to return to Madras for the final stages of my training, in the headquarters sections directly under the chief operations superintendent. i was more than a little worried about how things would go when I went to see my mother, but my sister Viola had been hard at work on my behalf and everything had settled down into a slightly uneasy calm. Mother was reconciled to my 'rebellion' especially as she soon discovered that Babs was expecting our first child.

Amrithraj joined me for the last leg of our training and we were intro-duced into the elevated world of policies and important decision taking. Then we had to endure a stiff examination, both written and oral, by the chief him-self, before we were formally advised that we had successfully completed our training and would be posted as assistant transportation superintendents (traf-fic). I was advised to report on 28 April 1948 to Guntakal to take up my posi-tion. My training had lasted for two years and six weeks.

I left Babs with her mother in Bangalore where it was arranged that she should have the baby and proceeded to Guntakal to take up my new job and move into my huge official quarters then furnished only with a camp bed and a small table. But it was a beginning.

The Railway Bridge over the Godavari River at Rajahmundry

Yvonne Marie Texeira (Babs), 1947

The author's wedding day, 1947

Assistant Transportation Superintendent: Guntakal District

I reported to Guntakal as instructed. The district traffic superintendent there was a Mr Chandy and I was to be his only assistant. As such I had responsibility, under him, for the commercial, operating, staff and even the stores, work on the district. There was no hard and fast dividing line, we each did everything that came up, but naturally I referred to him on all really important matters, especially those relating to the staff. At Guntakal there was also a district motive power superintendent, with an assistant; a district engineer with an assistant and a district medical officer. We lived in a circle of large official bungalows with the medical officer in the centre. One side of the railway track was reserved for the officers' quarters and the rest of the railway staff and the little town of Guntakal huddled on the other side. The station, the Catholic church and the Indian and European institutes were strategically located in the middle.

The Guntakal district was one of the smaller districts of the Madras & Southern Mahratta railway. It consisted of nearly 600 miles of exclusively metre gauge track, about 100 stations, depots, etc., and nearly 3000 traffic staff. The main line ran from the outer signal of Gadag in the west where we met the Hubli district, to Tadpalle just outside Bezwada in the east where we joined the Bezwada district. Guntakal was situated in the middle where the main broad gauge lines from Madras to Bombay crossed our district. Branch lines spread out from Hospet in the west to Kottur and Samehalli; from Bellary (the headquarters of the civil district), to Rayadurg; from Dronachellam down to Hindupur where we met the Mysore State Railways line to Bangalore; and from Guntur for 80 miles to Macherla. By Indian railway standards this was a small district but it was big enough and offered me experience of the whole range of railway work.

My quarters were the standard size for officers – simply huge. The compound was bare except for some trees running down from the gate to a circle in front of the entrance to the bungalow. A path led away from the compound into the area of the district offices. A wide veranda ran most of the way round the front and part of one side. Full-sized cloth and rattan 'chicks' shaded this, the sunny side of the building. A long living-room, a big square dining-room, and two large bedrooms complete with attached dressing-rooms and bathrooms made up the living quarters. Behind the dining-room was another trellis-enclosed veranda. Two pantries and a kitchenette flanked this veranda. The kitchen, garage and servants' quarters, all on an equally generous scale, were set back some way from the main building. Water was supplied from an overhead tank structure in the compound and a small water trough was to be found nearby. No, we did not have indoor plumbing but the bathroom was soon equipped with the usual zinc tub and 'thunder boxes' and a sweeper was always at hand to keep it clean.

I rattled around in this place until Babs, with a lot of help from her mother, filled the allotted two wagons with furniture, etc and despatched them from

Bangalore to Guntakal. There was her piano and piano stool; a wider than usual double bed which was fitted with two protective bars on one side to prevent the baby rolling off; a second and spare double bed; a dressing table, chest of drawers and wardrobe for the main bedroom, also a suitable assortment of mirrors; the dining-room table, chairs and serving table were of a suitable size; the drawing-room was furnished with a nice suite, plus occasional tables and extra cane chairs and tables for the veranda. Linen had been collected for a long time and crockery, cutlery and kitchen utensils were all easily obtained in Bangalore. In fact what we did not buy new was picked up cheap from the auction houses in Bangalore which had a constant turnover of good quality furnishings from the mobile population of this large military station.

The station master supplied me with labour from the tranship shed to convey my furnishings from the station, unpack and install everything in its right place. They were quite expert at all this. The loco shed sent along a few carriage cleaners who soon converted all the floors into shining ice-rinks. Labour was readily available to clear all the bushes and piles of rubbish in various corners of the garden, a very necessary task as the bag of snakes killed included one python, two cobras and a whole family of deadly kraits. I lurked safely in the rear of the workers but did step forward to crush the cobras, a task that the natives did not seem very keen to do. This was my second 'kill' as I had accomplished the same deed when staying with the Selvey family in Bezwada. I hate snakes and am simply terrified of them.

There is a story that I must tell at this stage. Once when I was training, I had to spend the night in a railway rest house and was a bit surprised when the caretaker, his staff and even my bearer, elected to sleep away from the bungalow. I put my torch and rattan cane down beside my bed and soon surrendered myself to a deep sleep. Then slowly I began to be aware that there was a strange smell in the room. If you have ever visited a snake house in a zoo you will quickly realise what had awakened me. One of my legs seemed to have gone dead on me and when I reached down for my torch and cane I discovered that they were on the opposite side of my camp bed and out of reach. I kept quiet for a while but dawn seemed to be far away and I had to do something so at last I summoned up my courage and eased out from my covering sheet and stood up. It was my 'dead side' and the torch and cane were still out of reach. I could feel what I thought was the triangular head of a snake below the foot of my useless leg. I stood for as long as I dared, silent and unmoving and as it grew lighter I glanced down to see – that I was standing with my good leg on the big toe of the numb foot. As I have said – I hate snakes!

Guntakal: My Quarters

The Indian 'Police Action' Against Hyderabad State

India achieved Independence and then proceeded to bully the Native States, which had never been part of British India but had remained independent entities bound by treaty to the crown. Hyderabad was the largest and perhaps the most wealthy of the Native States. The population was mainly Hindu but the Nizam and the large landowners were Muslims. All attempts at bullying failed and it was soon realised that Hyderabad was prepared to fight for its own independence. Guntakal district ran just south of the Hyderabad State Railway system. In fact our lines ran through their territory for a short distance between Guntakal and Hospet and their line ran down from Hyderabad to Kurnool Town and thence through Indian territory to Dronachellam, which lay on our main line east of Guntakal. While India prepared to invade the State I was asked by Chandy if I would take over the railway side of the operations from Guntakal district into Hyderabad. I pointed out that I was a British subject and completely neutral when it came to the sort of conflict that was being prepared. He would have to find somebody else to do the dirty work when it came to invading Hyderabad territory, but I would be quite happy to take over the railway operations from Dronachellam to Kurnool Town as that line, though operated by the Nizam's railway, lay completely within Indian territory. He was not very happy at that but could not argue the point openly because it was far too sensitive an issue.

Meanwhile the time when the baby should arrive was fast approaching and, of course, I could not be given any leave to go down to Bangalore to be near my wife. This was quite clear and so I settled down to drawing up comprehensive plans for the take-over of the Nizam's railway from Dronachellam to Kurnool Town. I was careful to get Chandy to sign every page of the plan and then sat back and waited for the balloon to go up.

As planned, the Indian Army invaded Hyderabad with mechanised divisions of crack troops from Bombay in the north. In the south only a holding operation was envisaged. Everything went according to the overall plan. The Hyderabad troops were quickly crushed in the north; only some irregular units recruited from the Pathan labour force working on the Tungabadra dam, east of Guntakal put up any sort of resistance until they too were over-run by the Gurkha regiments sent against them. Nothing happened on the Dronachellam – Kurnool Town sector. I took a special railway armoured train up the line, relieving the Nizam's railway staff and dropping off Guntakal district staff to take over their duties. As and when they were cleared by the Indian police, the Nizam's staff were brought back to their posts and my staff moved on further up the line. The Nizam's train services were cancelled and I brought in a temporary service on the Kurnool Town line to take its place. Everything was quiet and orderly until we reached the Kistna river at Kurnool. The Mysore Lancers were holding that sector but they could not get their bren gun carriers across the river. Their horses were almost useless in the heavy black cotton soil and although there was no action, they wanted their armoured vehicles to cross the river. We were told that there was a chance of civil rioting around the Nizam's mint at Munirabad, the very next station, and our help was urgently needed – just to cross the river. I could not really refuse and so we loaded the vehicles onto flat wagons and took them across. I was rather amused to find that the colonel of the Mysore Lancers, after a rather heavy dinner, was unable to turn the local maps right side up and had no idea of where he was. But that was none of our concern so we just hurried the task of unloading the trucks which was proving a much longer job than I had anticipated. Dawn broke before the last vehicle rolled off its truck and onto the track. Just then one of my inspectors drew my attention to some lorries from which men were being unloaded on the horizon. They seemed to be spreading out and when I drew the attention of the Mysore Lancer officers to this they almost threw a fit – the opposition had arrived. Shots were exchanged and at least one hit a steel rail wagon with a loud bang. This seemed to galvanise my chaps into action, in less time than it takes to relate, our special train was coupled up and we were heading away at top speed back across the river to Kurnool Town. That was the one and only time that I can claim to have been under fire!

The next day was taken up with railway work. The Kurnool line had to be connected to my control headquarters at Guntakal – a task for the signal and electrical engineers. Staff were clamouring to be fed and they claimed to be short of cash so I ordered them to be given meals free but each meal was recorded by their inspectors who would have to raise a debit against their pay – unless the railway in a bout of unaccustomed generosity waived the charge. Passengers continued to turn up at the railway stations all demanding to be taken further into India to Dronachellam or even Guntakal. What tickets were we to use and could we accept the Nizam's currency? Should any money so collected be sent back to Madras and under what security? I had to rule without delay and my answers were 'Yes, use the local tickets and accept the local currency'. A special service was arranged so that cash-collection chests were diverted for use on this 'new line'. The cashiers and even the audit office in Madras started to howl and an officer was sent up from Madras to review the position. He was my old friend Menon and when I asked him for any alternative suggestions his reply was simple – 'Carry on.'

The army meanwhile had found themselves unable to advance even a yard over the unfavourable terrain. Could we help – there was really no danger as the Nizam's forces had retreated over a hundred miles. The army was now faced with growing crowds of refugees all clamouring to be moved south into my territory. My reports from railway sources confirmed the position which was being aggravated as the Nizam's train services were reduced to ever shorter runs terminating nearer their own headquarters at the other end of the line. I first agreed to take a small reconnaissance party down the line on a trolley.

After about ten miles the trolley men were near collapse and the situation as reported was sufficiently confirmed. So I placed my saloon, inspection end leading, in front of the engine of my special train and with an army engineer to warn of mined tracks ahead I proceeded to run the army patrol as far as Mahbubnagar about 200 miles inside the Nizam's railway territory. There I stopped, at the river, and told the army that they would have to manage without any further help from me as my headquarters was screaming blue murder at what I had already done.

In five days the whole operation was over and Hyderabad had surrendered. I was amused to hear afterwards that one of my engine crews had yielded to the urgent pleas from the crew of a broken-down Nizam's engine and run their return service for them right back into Hyderabad itself. All hostilities were over and so the idiots were actually spotted shopping in the local bazaars while their engine was being turned round for the return journey. Quite a few railway staff, from Chandy down, were lectured by the new acting general manager, a nervous looking Brahmin, for exceeding their remit of responsibility. I do not know about the others but I'm afraid that it was all a bit of a lark so far as I was concerned. It was typical of the hypocrisy of the Indian government that the invasion and conquest of Hyderabad was called a 'Police action'. To me it was a naked use of superior force to subdue a small peaceful state that they wanted to annexe.

I was very careful to prepare a full report of every single thing that had happened and every action taken. For quite a few years I had great pleasure in referring all enquiries to my 'Secret Report'. To be truthful the real credit should go to the staff I had gathered around me for this exercise. They were superb. Everything was done correctly and a full record maintained at all times.

I should recount one incident that occurred before the invasion of Hyderabad. One afternoon I was informed by the control office that my brother was travelling on a train heading for Guntakal en route to Bombay. I was expecting my eldest brother Len to be on just such a journey to catch a ship for the UK and so I hurried to the station. No, there was no sign of him on the train but I was told that a couple of carriages were being shunted in the yard before being re-attached to the train. I wandered in search of them and coming upon a closely shuttered coach which seemed to fit the bill I hammered on the door, announced myself and called out to Len. A small corner of the shutters was opened and somebody replied that there was nobody named Stevenage in the compartment. The face seemed familiar and I at once recognised that here was the double of our Mr Chandy. I realised how the error had occurred. It was the district traffic superintendent's brother not the assistant traffic superintendent's brother who was on the train. I asked if he would like to speak to his brother but he hurriedly said 'No' and shut the window. I was not worried until – much later – our Mr Chandy explained that his brother was in the Indian Secret Service and had seized the personal letter from the Nizam of Hyderabad appealing for help from King George. He was taking it to Delhi where a duplicate would be made and passed on in due course. Meanwhile fearing that the British were after the original he had his revolver trained on me and had come pretty near to shooting me – a forerunner of James Bond! So much for the non-violent Indians.

Life In Guntakal

At last the news I was waiting for arrived, I had a little daughter born on 21 May 1948, exactly ten months after my marriage. I could not even get away for her christening on 31 May but it must have been quite obvious that I was not really fit for intelligent work and so I was granted leave for the first week-end in June and away I dashed to Bangalore to see Babs and the new miracle – my daughter. She was lovely and I swear that when I took her in my arms for the first time she actually smiled at me – obviously she had inherited good taste from her parents!

Babs and the baby were both well but obviously still not fit to join me in Guntakal. The week-end seemed to fly and I had to return to my desk leaving behind a hundred instructions that they should look after their health and not try to do too much too soon. Babs and I agreed that a nanny would be necessary, at least at first, and that steps should be taken to find a suitable girl for the job in Bangalore. We would later decide when they were ready for the move and I would come and escort them to Guntakal via Madras where I could show off my daughter to her grandmother and my sisters. Meanwhile I would try to be patient.

At last my patience was rewarded, Babs and little Patricia were ready to face the world at large. I got the necessary casual leave and armed with passes and a mountain of extra luggage, we were off to our own home. The stop-over at Madras was a great success. My mother greeted her latest grandchild with marked approval, my sisters made a fuss over her and Babs and I tried to hide my pride and joy, but failed.

Arrived safely in Guntakal, Babs set about rearranging her home and getting everything into the shape that suited her. The servants had slipped into lazy ways without a mistress to watch their work. The nanny was installed in the spare bedroom; the kitchen, ayah – cook and her little girl assistant were regularly inspected; the kitchen storeroom was re-stocked; the sweepers put a bit more effort into keeping the house clean and the bearer who had served me while I was training and had travelled around with me over the past two years decided that he would find life easier serving just another master rather than a house governed strictly by a watchful mistress. He went but we were not worried. I had the services of two official peons, one in the office and one for work at home and on line. It was the usual thing for the peon who looked after my office files etc. in my quarters to help out in the house and to look after not only the official work but also to cook for me when I was out on line.

Because Guntakal was such a long district and there was only one traffic assistant, either I or the district superintendent was usually out of the headquarters, at one end of the district or the other, (a journey of about twenty-four hours) and I spent more than half the month in my saloon inspecting stations, settling problems on the spot, carrying out investigations into accidents, complaints and reports of corruption and in general 'showing the flag' and keeping the staff on their toes. The railway officers' saloons were not only a luxury but a real necessity and as I controlled their allocation, mine was rather special and reserved only for me. I had a special box of cooking utensils, ingredients, cutlery, crockery and glasses always available in my saloon and a suitcase of clean clothes ready to be taken at a moment's notice to the station for my use on line.

The saloon consisted of a large living room which became an office when the desk was opened up, a dining table and chairs appeared seemingly out of nowhere when necessary, comfortably equipped bunks emerged at night and vanished into the woodwork during the day. The saloon had its own fully equipped bathroom and water supply and a further section was fitted out as a kitchen which also provided sleeping quarters for the cook. Yes, one could travel, and work, in considerable comfort for long periods. The saloon was usually parked in a quiet siding at night and picked up and moved from place to place by shunters who endeavoured never to disturb the occupant more than was absolutely necessary. The engines supplied hot water on demand; the peon/cook arranged with the local station masters for supplies of milk, eggs, fowls and fresh vegetables as required, conveyed all messages to and from the stations and most importantly, picked up the 'tappal' boxes filled with files which followed around by train wherever one went. So the routine of office work, papers to be read and signed, orders to be issued on files, all continued without interruption. When there were inter-departmental enquiries into accidents or other important matters, the concerned officers turned up each in his saloon and that made for pleasant social evenings when work could be forgotten until the next day. Sometimes I was able to take Babs and Patricia along with me in the saloon much to their delight and the obvious pleasure of the staff who all loved children and were sure that the Sahib would be in a better mood when his family was around and perhaps more lenient in his official dealings with them. Out came their wives and daughters and all the children to gather around the saloon and chat about families, food and of course, babies. It was certainly time for menfolk to find shelter in the office and work. But we seemed to leave a warm feeling behind us and so I took Babs and Patricia out with me whenever I could.

The saloon was fitted with glass windows all the way round and so I could admire the scenery as the train passed from black cotton lands, to the forests beyond Nandyal, to the hot tobacco growing fields around Guntur. The mountainous ghat sections were the most picturesque, high hills, deep ravines and green, dark green, trees. I remember well one night, when after a sharp rain shower the whole forest seemed to be lit by myriads of fireflies. I put out all the lights in the saloon and sat entranced by the passing forest of Christmas trees, brightly lit by flickering lights. On another occasion my saloon was attached to a goods train as we passed through the same forest area where a fire had taken control and flames leaped across the tracks from one side to the other. After consultation I agreed with the driver that if we backed up a bit and put on the maximum steam we could run the barrage of flames and get to the next station from which we could summon the forestry guards and fire-fighters whose presence had become vital to the containment of the fire which threatened disaster to a large forest of valuable timber. We did just that. It was really exciting.

Although there was plenty of game available and many amateur shikars ready to take a gun out in the hope of bagging birds, wild boar, deer and even big game, I did not indulge in the sport. I realised that I was absolutely useless with a gun. One evening when I was visiting Xavier, the assistant engineer at Guntur, I saw a magnificent tiger skin with a fully mounted head lying on the hearth in his lounge. I expressed my envy and he told me that this was the first and only tiger that he had shot and that I would be very welcome to come with him when he was next out shooting. Perhaps, if I was lucky, I would be able to bag a similar trophy. I gracefully declined and was very glad when I learned more details of his shooting technique. Xavier used to go out from Bogada across the dense forest to Chelema (two stations on the ghat section of my district) on the dark night of each month. He walked through the forest, alone, armed with a rifle and with a headlight attached to a helmet, much like a miner's headlamp. His eyesight was failing and he had begun to despair of ever bagging a tiger when one night he came across a fresh kill. He built a small shelter of stones as near as he dared and waited for the tiger to return to its half-eaten meal. It did, fortunately approaching from the safe side so that it did not get wind of him, and when he heard the crunch of bones under its great teeth he switched on his headlight and fired. The result lay there at my feet. Was I glad that I had refused his gracious offer to share his adventures?

The only time I actually saw tigers on my district is a story worth relating. When I was new to Guntakal and in the routine of checking the morning yard report of delays to mail trains, I spotted the explanation of a half hour delay at Bogada due to 'tigers on the track'. I did not quite believe the story but when it appeared again the next night I felt that some action was called for. An 'official explanation' was called for, and when the same story was repeated I first warned the station master and when the same thing happened again I suspended him and then fined him. Then I went out on line into the area, attached my saloon just behind the engine and then moved over to ride with the driver on his engine. I asked him whether the staff at Bogada were just trying it on because I was the new boy. He replied that the story I had been told was indeed true and offered to prove it. Some distance before we reached Bogada he switched off his headlight and coasted the train toward the station. The outer signal was at danger and as we knew, the signal lever to operate the same was at the foot of the home signal. The driver asked for my authority to pass the signal at danger which I gave and so he quietly coasted on towards the home signal. Then he switched on his headlight, blew his whistle and speeded into the station blowing clouds of steam. To my surprise I saw a family of tigers jump up from the foot of the home signal and dash towards the surrounding jungle. What nobody had told the 'new boy' was that a water column was situated at the home signal and drips usually formed a little pool at the foot of the signal. Tigers from the surrounding forest found this a convenient watering hole and no member of the station staff in his right mind would venture out at night to pull the signal lever located almost in the pool. All the drivers on the route knew the problem and blew their whistles and scared away the tigers before approaching the station when the staff dashed out with lamps and loud clamour to lower the signal for the train to enter the station area. Delays were inevitable. I went back to my office much chastened. I apologised to the station master, reinstated him to normal duties, removed the offending entry in his service record and refunded the fines imposed. Mea culpa, Mea maxima culpa!

In March 1997 while I was revisiting India after an interval of nearly fifty years I was astounded by a graphic reminder of this experience. I was in the veranda bar of the Taj Bengal Hotel in Calcutta – a very plush place – when I spotted a picture on the wall of the bar which depicted a family of tigers fleeing before a steam engine which approached them and a signal column at full speed, puffing steam in all directions while the driver and others on the footplate leaned out to enjoy the spectacle. Although I tried to recognise myself on the footplate that would have been too much of a coincidence!

My only other contact with shikar was my enjoyment of the customary joint which was presented to all the seniors in the headquarters when somebody in the railway colony took out his gun and bagged a suitable deer from the comfort of his trolley as it was pushed along the line almost in sight of the headquarters station.

The social life of a railway headquarters centered around the Railway Institutes. There was a separate institute for Indian staff and another for European and Anglo-Indian staff. These presented the usual opportunities for tennis, cricket, hockey and football. The European Institute had regular dances and everybody found something to amuse and interest them when the weather was kind – not too hot and not too rainy. The district traffic superintendent was president of the European Institute and I, his assistant, was president of the Indian Institute. I think that this had a lot to do with our control over special leave and passes, essential ingredients for any away fixtures. Babs and I loved dancing and tried never to miss a dance at the Institute. We were fairly good and I remember, with pride, that on one occasion, at least, the dancers cleared the floor and allowed us what could be termed an exhibition dance. There were other occasions when a number of the staff at Guntakal made up a party to go to a dance at Bellary, some thirty miles along the line. It was usually possible to arrange an appropriate 'test run' for the 'accident special train' and everybody co-operated by attaching their official saloons to the special so that the party could travel in comfort, change into suitable clothing en route and get some sleep on the way back after a happy evening out.

Visits from other members of the officers' colony and the managers of Ralli Brothers and Volkarts, two of the large commercial enterprises that operated in the area were our main social engagements. Of course the Dutch parish priest and his assistant were regular visitors and enjoyed many an evening in our company.

Father Van der Reit, the parish priest of St Ann's Catholic church was a dear old man who could drink straight gin with you all evening, stop just before midnight and still be fit to preach a long sermon at early mass the next morning. It was some time after my arrival in Guntakal that I discovered that my parents had been married in St Ann's on 18 February 1903. Mother told me that her father – Michael Norman Rylands – was the assistant medical officer at the Railway Hospital in Guntakal and that they had lived in the little railway bungalow near the hospital, almost in the shadow of the large overhead water tank which supplied the station and probably kept them cool. Dad, fresh out of the Madras Medical College, was the Indian Medical Department's military doctor of the prison camp at Bellary, which held a large number of Boer prisoners-of-war far away from their homes in South Africa. I suppose that it was their medical background and the fact that Dad was educated in the same college as her father that brought them together. Father Van der Reit gave me a copy of their marriage certificate to add to my growing collection of genealogical records. I had always wondered where Dad had picked up his smattering of Dutch and here was the answer. Mother showed me a lovely little brooch made of bone and carved with her name in a wreath of flowers. She explained that this was the wedding gift made for her by the Boer prisoners-of-war in Bellary.

Father Piet, the assistant at Guntakal was a happy young man and when you got him to talk he was very enthusiastic about athletics and had a fund of stories about his dealings with the Dutch resistance movement in Amsterdam during the war. He had carried messages between the various resistance groups and had even helped to move escaped prisoners-of-war and Jews along the 'underground railway' operated by the resistance. No, he had not met or heard of Anne Frank – had anybody at that time? When I heard that the film of the 1948 Olympic Games was showing at Guntur I mentioned it to Father Piet and he was so keen to see it that he got leave of absence from his superior and I took him down the line in my saloon to Guntur where he specially enjoyed the feats

Hampi: The fabled city of Vijayanagar

The Monolithic ratha or Stone Chariot, in front of the Vijayavittala Temple in Hampi

of Fanny Blankers-Koen, the Dutch housewife who won four gold medals – the 100 metres, the 200 metres, the 80 metres hurdles and then anchored the Dutch women to a handsome win in the sprint relay. He was thrilled and could not stop talking about the film and the Dutchwoman's success for weeks.

One of my tasks on the district was to accompany visiting dignitaries when they toured our area by rail. In this way I met Vallabhai Patel, the strong-man of the Congress party and now a real power in government. He was very silent that day as he was suffering from an asthma attack and reserved his strength and voice for his public meetings. The chief government inspector of railways, a new man in the post, wanted to visit the ruins of Hampi which were located just a few miles away from Hospet on our district. When I offered to help with his arrangements he declined and said that everything had been planned by his staff and added that unfortunately the numbers could not be extended to in-clude me. I had heard a lot about Hampi, the vast ruins of the once mighty Vijayanagar kingdom which fell to Ali Adil Shah and his Muslim forces in 1565. I had always meant to visit the place and this seemed the perfect occa-sion. The station master at Hospet arranged a car and a guide – one of his many relatives – and off I went armed with a full hamper of goodies for lunch. The ruins were every bit as majestic and wonderful as I had heard and I spent hours wandering all over the miles and miles of stone buildings, statues, empty bath-ing tanks and fallen temples. The Muslims had spent years trying to remove every trace of the Hindu kingdom that had resisted them so long. They did a good job on most of the temples but left enough untouched to convince any later visitor that here indeed had stood a mighty kingdom and a flowering civi-lisation. I regret to say that the chief government inspector of railways was ill-served by his guide and soon joined me and my guide who, being a local man, really knew his way around. When we all got back to the station I learned that there had been a bad accident at Ongole on the north eastern line of the Madras & Southern Mahratta railway. Two trains had smashed head-on into each other just off the platform where a number of passengers were waiting for their train. One of the engine boilers had blown up and there was a heavy loss of life. I informed the chief inspector and asked if he would like me to arrange for his broad gauge saloon waiting at Guntakal to be turned ready for the fast train to Madras and onward movement to Ongole. He said that it was 'not necessary' but later on that night woke me with a query whether I could make the sug-gested arrangements without heavy delay to trains. He gave me an odd look when I replied that I had already acted as suggested because I had realised that with the many deaths reported he, the most senior officer on the railways, would have to hurry to the scene. He even thanked me for my help but I do not know what, if anything, he put on my service report.

Patricia was growing up, a lovely, lively, talkative child. When I had to escort the new Indian Governor of Madras on a trip around my district I took

Babs and Patricia with me. One morning, I think it was on the second day of the tour, the liveried chauffeur was wiping down the luxurious Government House car near where my saloon was parked, it had been covered with rose garlands. He did not realise that he had a very interested little watcher until she called out to him asking what he was doing. He ignored her but she was certainly not going to stand any nonsense from him. 'Dirty car, it stinks' was her loud comment and the chauffeur was seen jumping up and down in righteous indignation when Babs removed our critical daughter from the scene.

Patricia had indeed grown up and Babs soon agreed that she could manage without the nanny and with only a little help from an ayah. So off went the nanny to Bangalore without many regrets on either side. Now we were free to have guests in the spare bedroom suite she had occupied. My sister Therese had recently lost her first child and was taking it rather badly. We invited her and Noel to have a short holiday with us and thought that it might help her a bit if we practically handed Patricia over into her care for the duration of the holiday. It seemed to work, she came alive again and one might even think that Patricia had helped because she conceived her son, Christopher, shortly after this holiday.

My sister Viola, her son Trevor and his ayah, also spent a short holiday with us. The ayah had been allowed to get too much of her own way by Viola who did not seem able to control her servants. The ayah soon realised that I would stand no nonsense and I think that she must have breathed a sigh of relief when after a happy holiday Viola decided that it was time to return to Madras. It was lovely to be able to repay, even in such a small way, the great help my favourite sister had been to me in the difficult days after my marriage.

Babs wanted to go down to Bangalore to attend the wedding of her friend and cousin Barbara Bridle to Melville Gaughan. Although I regretted the loss of my family even for so short a time, it was something that was important to Babs and so off she went with the baby and big plans for shopping expeditions with her mother in Bangalore where the choice of luxuries and necessities was great and the prices not excessive. Somebody caught a chill and the short trip was extended to a month much to my disappointment.

Meanwhile my job continued to hold my imagination and interest and I could quite happily lose myself in the control office for hours on end. The staff and commercial sectors of my work were equally demanding but the operations side of things was what interested me most. I just loved playing with real trains. While my family was away in Bangalore, south India was struck by exceptionally severe storms and all the lines running to the north were breached by swollen rivers. What were just trickling streams one day, overnight became raging torrents sweeping away embankments, bridges and girders. It happened that a district officers' enquiry had taken all the district officers to a section of our line which became isolated and they were completely cut off from all contact with their offices in Guntakal. I was left as the senior officer in the headquarters (except for the medical officer) and for nearly three days and nights I practically lived in the control office directing the movement of all traffic. The main line broad gauge trains to Delhi, to Bombay and to Calcutta were all interrupted and I took all of them, transhipped passengers and goods at Guntakal into metre gauge stock and moved them via Dronachellam to Hyderabad on the Nizam's railway where they were transhipped back again into broad gauge stock and moved north, clear of all the flooding.

At the end of this period, just before the district officers returned to head-quarters, Mr Reed the general manager came to see us. On the same train Madras despatched Mr Saldanah, a senior officer, to take charge of Guntakal. But Reed was having none of that, he ordered Mr Saldanah back to Madras and instructed me to attach my saloon behind his as he toured the district. I was also instructed to get some sleep as he did not want to see me again until we returned to Guntakal. I fell into my bunk and went out like a light for over twenty-four hours. When I presented myself before him again at Guntakal he gave me a good look and started to question me about all that had occurred while I was in charge. I got the distinct impression that I passed with flying colours! We got onto more general topics and he was particularly interested when I claimed that the system of allocating engines and brake vans to sectors of the district was flawed. I showed him a chart I had prepared which proved that because of the variation of engine hauling capacity and brake van controlling capacity over the differing gradients of the sectors, there could be only one system of allocating engines and brake vans to the sectors which would reduce to a minimum the wastage of power of both engines and brakes. Yes, he agreed with me, and made a note to raise the subject at the earliest opportunity. Needless to say nothing had changed when I left India.

I seemed to be getting quite a reputation as a trains operator. At one stage the chief operations superintendent at the Madras headquarters expressed his surprise at the growth of the outstanding demand for wagons for loading merchandise on my district. I tried to tell him that the demand was inflated by merchants who were ordering wagons before they had the necessary goods to load into them. He sounded doubtful and I felt obliged to prove my theory. By restricting loading for a week or so and by hiding away suitable wagons in unexpected sidings I built up a full train load of empties. The system was that stations would be instructed every morning to load available wagons with merchandise on offer taking into account the order of government priority allotted to the type of goods concerned. If wagons were not loaded by the traders when made available a fine of Rs50 per wagon was imposed upon the offending trader. Early one morning I produced my train load of empties at the western end of my district and ordered the stations to load all outstanding demands in strict order of priority, but the order was to exhaust all outstanding demands at a station before the empties were moved on to the next station. The inflated demand for wagons was exposed. The traders paid the fines and a wave of cancellations of demand before allocation spread down the line. I set a rumour running that I had a similar train of empties ready in the east of the district and the cancellations grew apace. When the chief examined the yard report the next morning he could not believe his eyes. The outstanding demand for wagons on my district had more than halved. He wanted to know how this had happened and could only laugh when I explained how I had proved my theory and corrected the situation.

We started to get quite a lot of trouble from Communist terrorists who infiltrated our district from Hyderabad and almost every night there were reports of trains being derailed by obstructions on the track and spikes being placed in the rail joints. Then they started to use dynamite on the track and things got more serious. The nightly disturbances grew so frequent that I gave the control orders that I was only to be called out in the event of loss of lives. A telephone call in the middle of the night still has me starting out of bed with all my nerves jangling.

On one occasion when I was touring the line near Guntur, my saloon was attached to the engine of a freight train and consequently given priority over the late-running passenger train which would normally enter the block section outside Guntur at about that time. Suddenly there was a loud explosion. Our engine was lifted into the air together with the front of my saloon but fortunately both landed safely back on the rails. Everybody jumped down from the engine and from the guards van and I joined them in searching for the cause of the explosion. We soon discovered a bundle of sticks of dynamite half hidden in bushes near the track. The bombers had been aiming to blow up the passenger train but had been disturbed by the unexpected arrival of our freight train. They hurried their job and had time only to jam one stick of dynamite between the joints of the rails. This was indeed fortunate for us. I picked up the rest of the explosives and for lack of any other safety measures immersed them in a tub of water in my bathroom and told the driver to make all speed to Guntur so that we could alert the police to the fact that a terrorist gang was in the vicinity. They appeared in due course, carefully took charge of the dynamite and failed to find any terrorists.

About this time we got a new district traffic superintendent at Guntakal. Terence Ryan had spent all his service in the general manager's office but when his cousin Mr Crawford became chief commercial manager of the Madras & Southern Mahratta railway, Ryan was given his chance to run a district. The week-end before he arrived Crawford visited Guntakal and in the most tactful manner explained to me that whereas Ryan would be in charge I would be held personally responsible if anything went seriously wrong. That was all right. Terence and his wife were nice folk, good Catholics, childless but friendly with everybody. I set up a quiet system with the office superintendent that all orders passed by the district traffic superintendent had to be shown to me before they were issued and that he was never to know of my action. It worked and there were relatively few 'order files' that vanished into my locked cabinet 'unavoidably missing or delayed'. After a few months I applied for ten days casual leave. Ryan climbed on his high horse and wanted to know why I wanted to take leave. I explained that that was strictly my business but relented enough to tell him that I wanted to take my little family on a pilgrimage to the church of Our Lady of Velankanni in thanksgiving for the safe arrival of my beloved daughter. He gave in but his response seemed to be grudging so I told him how I had been keeping a watchful eye on all his work since his arrival and had saved him from several rather serious errors. This I explained, tongue in cheek, was at the express wish of the chief commercial manager. As he grew more and more angry, I called for all the hidden files and explained exactly the trouble he would have been in if his orders had been allowed to pass unobstructed. He did not like what I had done but when I suggested that he was now free to alter the date and promulgate his orders he quickly cooled down. I got my leave without further argument and he gradually became less high and mighty and more friendly. Babs, Patricia and I went to Velankanni and gave thanks for her safe delivery. Then we came back to a more relaxed office where Ryan was happy to discuss things with me rather than dash off orders without knowing the background to the cases before him. My chief commercial clerk, whose brother had made arrangements for our stay at Velankanni reported back that I was very fluent in Tamil, something that Subramaniam and indeed none of the office had previously known. One evening when Ryan and his wife were visiting us Patricia was given a plate of sweets to hand round. Ryan looked at it and said, 'How nice, I like these, I shall have two'. He was surprised when my little daughter stood her ground and said in a loud voice, 'You can only take one at a time, the second one only after you have finished the first'. He turned red with embarrassment while his wife roared with laughter and seriously told him that Patricia was quite right and he had to put the second sweet back. He did so and the little terror placed the plate on a table close to him and skipped away full of righteousness. Poor Ryan, he was soon transferred away from Guntakal to a bigger district – Hubli – but on his next home leave fell sick on the voyage home, died and was buried at sea.

The Changing Climate Of Work In India

Things were happening in India which proved that life would be very different for Europeans and Anglo-Indians under a Hindu majority government. The pressure for everybody to pass the Hindi language examinations increased. I only got through by the skin of my teeth, mainly by fast talking, in Tamil, to the examining officer – a Tamilian. My opposite number on the Hubli District, fell foul of the railway unions and found himself locked up in the police cells of his headquarters station. A false accusation had been laid against him and it took us nearly five days to prove the clear falsity of the complaint and get him released. Needless to say his railway career was ruined. One of my predecessors at Guntakal, Hugh Gordon got himself appointed harbour superintendent at Mombasa. Hooper, the district traffic superintendent at Bezwada resigned and was last heard of as the yard master at Medicine Hat in Canada. The signs were there for all to read. We had the best jobs and there were many people more than eager for these appointments.

Meanwhile the Stevenage families had made up their collective and several minds. My brother Len and his family had departed for England. Val, my second brother, completed his twenty-one years service in the Army Medical Establishment, came to Madras and picked up mother and sailed for the UK to start a new life. His wife and children left just before him to set up home in York where he had fixed himself up with a job in the local hospital. Mother had predicted that where she, an old and sick lady, could go her children should not be afraid to follow.

I set about getting my papers together and proving my right to British citizenship and a British passport. I applied for my allocated quota of privilege leave and went to Bombay with Val and mother to wish them luck in their new venture.

Bombay was worth the visit and I drank in all the sights knowing that I might never have another chance to look around this busy industrial city. It was with more than a suspicion of tears in my eyes that I watched my indomitable mother refuse all aid and climb slowly up the gangway onto the deck of the ship which was to take her away from India for the rest of her life.

Babs was in Bangalore, with her mother, and on my return there I found that a complication had arisen to bedevil our plans. She was pregnant. I was delighted at the prospect of another child – maybe a son – but that could upset the delicate timing of our plans to leave India and join the growing family in the UK. Meanwhile my leave expired and I was unexpectedly posted back to Guntakal. That made parting from the railways even harder to contemplate. But I pushed ahead. Citizenship papers and passports were secured for me, for Babs and for Patricia. I tried unsuccessfully to get a redundancy package from the railways but failing that put in my resignation with effect from 14th November 1950. The customary month's notice was given and I set about trying to fix a cheap and early passage to the UK.

Thomas Cook offered me just that, a berth on the *Chusan* leaving Colombo on 20th December 1950. Babs was very upset at the thought of my going on ahead and having to follow later with the children. But we agreed that this was the only course open to us and I wrote accepting the offered passage. I posted it in the post box at the office but when I got back home Babs was in such a state that I asked my office superintendent to stand by the box and re-cover my letter when the postman came to clear the box. Such things were possible in India and in due course the letter came back to me. I handed it to Babs to be destroyed saying that I would write another the next day. Then I went for my bath and when I came out I discovered that Babs had steeled herself and come to a decision. She took the letter and posted it herself in the main post office box.

There was such a lot to be done. Some part of our household goods was sold locally at Guntakal. Linen and items of clothing etc, were packed for transport to Bangalore. A letter to the High Commissioner asking for my next child's name, a blank at present, to be inserted on Bab's passport, was drafted and Thomas Cooks were asked to try for another passage for my wife and children after a suitable interval. There were the usual farewell parties, presentations of garlands (mine was a rather special affair of gold and silver thread), formal addresses and speeches at Guntakal and in the rush of things happening I hardly had time to reflect on the gravity of the step I was taking. I was giving up a good position; going to a new country to try and find another job; leaving my wife and children to follow; and all this with hardly any money, and no contacts other than my mother and my brothers in the UK. Looked at in retrospect it was an awesome decision. But the die was cast. I asked for my Provident Fund balance to be paid into my bank account which was transferred so that Babs could operate it freely; it was small enough by any standards. Viola came to my assistance again and presented me with all the spare cash she had and also arranged for me to stay with a friend of hers in Colombo for the short time between my arrival from India and my scheduled departure for the UK.

We spent the last weeks in Bangalore with Babs' mother and step-father trying not to face the inevitable fact that the date for my departure was coming ever nearer. It arrived and I steeled myself into a dry-eyed goodbye but dissolved in tears as the train steamed out of Bangalore cantonment. In Madras there was Viola to help and Therese and Noel planning their own departure. I found time to visit Dad's grave and was surprised to find that somehow our old servants, the ayah, the chauffeur and the cook had discovered my plans and were already there to bid me farewell. Our servants were more than just that, they were truly our friends.

Our Lady of Velankanni

Ceremonial garlands presented to the author on his departure from India

118

G. 41 (Book)

MADRAS AND SOUTHERN MAHRATTA RAILWAY

SERIAL No.............. **59**

CERTIFICATE OF SERVICE

............*Madras*...STATION *Chief Operating Supdt's* OFFICE

......*7th November*..195D

PARTICULARS

1. Name...*Mr. P. H. Stevenage*......
2. (1) Father's Name...*Capt. E. A. Stevenage*..2. (2) Caste...*Christian (Catholic)*
3. Date of Birth...*7th June 1922*.............................
4. Identification marks (if any).......—.........................
   ....
5. Department in which employed...*Operating (Traffic)*...............
6. Period of Service From...*11-3-1946*...To...*13-11-1950*.........
7. Appointment when leaving Service...*Assistant Transportation Supdt (Traffic)*
8. Rate of Pay on leaving Service...*B. 380/- p.m.*:...............
9. Reasons for leaving Service...*Resigned*.........................
   ....
   ....
10. Conduct...*Good*....
11. Abilities......*Good*.....
    ....
12. Time keeping...*Good*..

13. Employee's Signature or Thumb Print   *[signature]*

Department...*Operating*.........   Signature..........*[signature]*

                                        Designation...*Chief Oplg. Supdt.*

To

P. H. Stevenage Esq., M. A.,

ASSISTANT TRANSPORTATION SUPERINTENDENT, (TRAFFIC),

M. & S·M· Rly. GUNTAKAL·

SIR

On the eve of your relinquishing your office as Assistant Transportation Superintendent on this Railway, We, the staff of The Transportation (Traffic), Guntakal have assembled here this evening to bid you FAREWELL.

Your term of office as Asst. Trans Supdt. was a period of great activity in the annals of Guntakal District History. One amongst the many is the Hyderabad Police action. The consequent strain imposed on our Railway rested lightly on your shoulders. You rallied round you a band of young men, infused spirit and courage into them and marched ahead undaunted to the forefront in carrying out the mandates given to you. Young in age and spirit, courageous and ever cheerful, with a rare gift of leadership and ability to handle any situation with ease and grace, you have proved a great source of inspiration to us all. Guntakal District had the unique honour and privilege of enjoying and serving you, during your full term of office on the Railway as Asst Trans. Supdt.

Your charming and amiable manners and the kind consideration you always showed to the staff at all times have made you popular and contributed not a little in establishing ESPRIT DE CORPS amongst the members of your staff.

We are sorry you are leaving us, but we console ourselves at the happy thought that you are going to England to join your dear Mother, to fulfil a desire uppermost in your heart. Sir, wherever you may go and whatever office you may hold, you are sure to make a mark in life.

May the Giver of All grant you, Mrs. and Baby Stevenage best of life, health, wealth and happiness and many many opportunities, by which, YOU, with your abilities, will easily climb the ladder of life and prosperity which you so richly deserve.

We wish you, BON VOYAGE, BRIGHT FUTURE, and BEST OF LUCK. ADIEU. Sir,

GUNTAKAL

12....11....50

We beg to remain,
Faithfully yours,

TRANSPORTATION TRAFFIC STAFF.
(Guntakal District.)

Sri Vittal Press Guntakal

Address on the author's departure

120

P. & O. 'CHUSAN'

TOURIST PUBLIC ROOMS

Farewell To India: A Fresh Start

On 20th December, Dad's birthday, the *Chusan* steamed out of Colombo taking me to a new and very different life.

The *Chusan* was scheduled to stop at Bombay, Aden, Port Said and then sail straight on to Tilbury. I had said my 'goodbye' to India and so I did not get off the ship there; at Aden I went ashore with a party from the ship and wandered around the area of the Crater in a sort of a daze. I must confess that that was exactly how I felt – nothing seemed real to me. There I was sailing away from my family and my home to a new country where everything would be different. I had no job to go to and my sole wealth was fifty pounds. Soon it was Christmas Day and then the New Year arrived. Nobody was allowed ashore at Port Said because we were having trouble with the Egyptians about the Canal. There was the expected round of holiday fare, dancing and concerts but all I could do was worry about the welfare of my wife and the expected birth of our baby; worry too about my future in England. No, I cannot say that it was a happy voyage but it came to an end with no telegram about the baby and no resolution of any of my worries.

I stood on the deck on a cold, misty morning and watched as the ship entered Torbay to pick up letters and papers. Then we sailed on to Tilbury where all was bustle until we were landed complete with our luggage. Mother had arranged for Len to meet me on arrival and see me onto the train for St Pancras, London. It was wonderful to see his smiling, well-known face and to realise that there were some people in this new land who were friends and relatives. At St Pancras I was surprised to be met by my cousin Kitty Kelly, another of my mother's little arrangements. She saw me through the transfer from St Pancras to Kings Cross and onto a train for York. I sat in a comfortable, warm train and looking out of the window had my first sight of snow. Then wonder of wonders, we stopped at a station called Stevenage! Things were beginning to look better and when we reached York there was my sister-in-law, Dolly, to greet me, take me to the hospital where my brother Val worked and then on to their home where I was greeted by my mother with her accustomed warmth and love. All was well with me, I was in the bosom of my family and nothing could go wrong.

I spent a couple of weeks in York where I received a telegram announcing the birth of my son Michael and the glad news that mother and child were both doing fine. Mother had saved up a little of her small pension and she passed that on to me and I opened a bank account with Lloyds. Then it was time to find a job and that was best done from London. My cousin, Edgar Platel, lived in 'digs' in Croydon, with another school friend of ours, Dick Reynolds and his family. He arranged for me to share with him, met me at Euston and off we went to Croydon and the second adventure – finding a job.

British Railways

I got daily copies of the newspapers, examined them carefully and sent out dozens of applications for likely-looking jobs. But either I had misjudged the type of work for which I was applying or else I was not applying in an acceptable manner but I grew more and more despondent as the weeks went by and my money slowly vanished. Edgar had found work as a clerk on the railways and in the end that was where I had to turn for my first job.

I asked about traffic apprenticeships and was told that I was over the age limit for the scheme in operation at the time. But, just for that year, I fell under the age limit for applicants from the railways staff for an apprenticeship. That offered me some hope so I joined the staff of the London Midland & Scottish Railway as a clerk, Class 5, the lowest of the lowly clerical grades. I was posted to the yard-master's office at Willesden which I discovered was quite a distance from Croydon, but there it was, my first job in England.

I let a couple of months go by and then asked about the traffic apprenticeship scheme. The lists had closed earlier that month.

I still tried to secure a better job outside the railways but met with no success at all. I decided that I had to rise in the railway world where every aspect of the work was familiar to me. So I started to apply for almost every item that appeared on the internal vacancy lists. In the operating field the emphasis was all on practical local experience but the accounts departments had vacancies which they were prepared to fill from any applicants who had some sort of accounting knowledge and ability. So I got my first promotion to the acquisitions division of the British Transport Commission. I was now a clerk Class 4. But in the railways world the organisation was in a state of flux. Nationalisation of all transport under the Transport Commission was changing to denationalisation under a Railways Board for the rail elements of transport. Acquisitions ended and I was made redundant. But it was not long before I was promoted into the audit division of the Railways Board – Clerk, Class 2. The lower rungs of a ladder are usually dusty and difficult but I was determined and I spent the next eleven years auditing.

I am often asked how I coped with life in post-war England. The answer is really quite well. At first I did miss not having servants to do all the daily chores but I soon got over that and knuckled down to doing everything without turning around for assistance. I learned to watch how people around me managed their lives and quickly followed suit. The fact that my family and so many of my friends were also adjusting to 'the new life' did help with lots of practical examples.

I found that everyone I met responded to politeness and people went out of their way to help with information and directions. At work there was the usual tussle of competition for promotion but I never encountered the sort of downright cheating that we had all come to expect in India.

THE ASSOCIATION OF CERTIFIED AND CORPORATE ACCOUNTANTS

INCORPORATED 1905

This is to Certify

that *Patrick Hugh Stevenage*

of *Haywards Heath*

was admitted a

Fellow of the Association

on the 29th day of September 1970.

Admitted an Associate 24th, April, 1961.

Given under the Seal of the Association

this 24th day of November 1970.

E. Lediard Smith
Member of the Council

John Ambrose
Member of the Council

T. Cameron Osborne
Secretary

THIS CERTIFICATE IS THE PROPERTY OF THE ASSOCIATION

124

The British Railways Board Headquarters, Marylebone Road, London,
now an hotel

Patricia and Michael (2 eldest children) c1957 in India

The cold weather was something I had never experienced before, but I had warm clothes. I plunged happily into the snow and carefully trod the icy pavements. I even safely negotiated the dreaded London smog of 1952/3 when people held hands as they walked along the pavements to and from work. Unlike in India, work did not stop for such things as bad weather or natural hazards.

Meanwhile I was having trouble with the family in India. Babs would not agree to stay with any of my family in England and insisted that we should have a place of our own. To arrange this months before she arrived would be impossible. I coaxed her friend Pam Owen with whom I was now in digs to offer her accommodation but this too was unacceptable. Meanwhile the money I had left with her in India was fast running out and I had to send her a monthly allowance which if small was all that I could afford. I quite understood that she was reluctant to face the voyage to the UK with two little children and to face the prospect of having to shop, cook, clean and do all the housework which she had servants to do for her in her mother's home in India. But we had faced all this before we made our decisions and it seemed to me that the only thing wrong was that I had failed to get a good job straight away in England and failed to get enough money for her to live in the sort of comfort that was still available in India. I stuck this for as long as I could and then laid down an ultimatum. I would book passages from this end and pay for them but she must accept the booking and come or else I would institute divorce proceedings. I would do my best but I could not accept any further prevarication or conditions. The day the shipping company confirmed the booking to her she cancelled it. I told my solicitor to go ahead with securing a divorce which he did. Much to our surprise the judge awarded me custody of the children, leaving them for the time being in her care and protection. I paid her a monthly allowance as laid down by the court for the maintenance of the children. It was all far from satisfactory. The children wrote monthly letters, stiff and angry. As indeed we all were.

I was more than determined to succeed in my job and pressed ahead with my efforts to secure an accounting qualification. As I was in full time employment I had to do this through a correspondence course and that took me four years, from 1957 to 1961. I got my qualification and the doors to promotion in the finance departments of the Board opened to me. But still I wanted my family with me and eventually, after her mother's death, Babs decided that she had better come to the UK and bring the children under the direct jurisdiction of British courts. I promised that I would never seek to take them away from her. I did not want to start a tug of war for their affections – one which I seemed certain to lose. So they came in March 1961 and I found them a flat in Croydon. I tried to effect a reconciliation but that proved impossible and she moved away to live near her cousins in Essex.

127

Anne Hazel Stevenage, the author's present wife, 1963

At the Board there was always a round of holidays, dances and parties and because I was safely married I found myself a reserve partner for the young ladies who were between boy friends or had quarrelled with them temporarily. The only difficulty was that I was always short of cash and could never consider the expensive sort of holidays they planned or some of the theatre or concert visits. Anyway I had not been looking for romance outside my marriage and remained hopeful that somehow all would be well once Babs and the children were close at hand in England. When I was forced to accept that there was no hope for this I found that happiness awaited me just around the corner and I wooed and won Anne Hazel Barthels who consented to become my bride. We were married in March 1963 and in due course had two lovely children, Hugh, in 1965 and Sarah in 1968.

But before the birth of Hugh my mother died in the General Hospital at Croydon on 22 October 1963. She suffered a cerebral thrombosis while recovering from a painful fall and a broken leg. My mother loved all her children with a great and enduring love but I must confess that perhaps she did keep that little bit extra for me, her youngest child. She was the rock on which my whole life was built. She was always on my side, no matter what happened. Her greatest pride was in my achievements and so how could I ever put anything but my best effort into everything I attempted. I am glad that she saw me on the high-road to success in my job in England and happy in my marriage. I am sure that she would have loved to see the children of that happiness – Hugh and Sarah. With her passing the days of my youth ended, everything that came after seemed somehow incomplete because I could not present it to her to share… and approve.

Meanwhile happiness in my home life had the effect of removing the chip that I had carried for years on my shoulder. I relaxed in my job and promotions came more frequently. I eventually got back to the level I had left in India but at a much higher salary. For eleven years I had audited accounts and my job was to find errors in the figures and in the accounting procedures. The next four years, from 1967 to 1971, was spent in creating new railway accounting systems suitable for the world of computers. I did not touch the dreaded machines but I set out what the programmers had to achieve, then got in our internal auditors to test the systems, almost to destruction, and if they passed that test then I brought in teams of accounting staff to install the systems and train the staff in their use. To modernise cash control we introduced cash registers into the system for the first time on British Rail. After five years of work in development sections I was told that I had outstripped the available time scale for development and that I should move on. It seemed appropriate to all concerned that I should spend a little time with our financial consultancy subsidiary company – 'Transmark'. This took me to Portugal and then to the Sudan but I did not relish living out of a suitcase and grabbed the first opportunity to return to my regular job. My final move was into the section which vetted the financial case presented by the various departments to the Board and then to the Transport Department of the Government to secure finances for the new works to be introduced into the railway systems. I also had to monitor the investment budget of the Railways Board, some four hundred million pounds per annum. This was a really challenging job and I was required to attend every meeting of the investment committee of the board which was chaired either by the chairman or the chief executive of the board. Mine was the final financial opinion voiced and the chairman once said that the committee could overrule me when it was felt necessary, but they had no right to stop me voicing my opinion. There were many arguments which I won and some which I lost but this was the final rung of the ladder of my success. I rewrote the investment manual of the board and got it approved by the Department of Transport. There was nothing more left for me to aim at within reason.

We bought a nice home in Haywards Heath and I settled down in comfort and happiness to see through my service until early retirement was offered me in 1983 and gratefully accepted. The railways were going to be denationalised and sold off to the highest bidder. It was time for me to go.

One other joy had come to me as I relaxed in my new found happiness. My son Michael found me again and made friends. He was delighted to learn that he had a brother and baby sister. He brought Patricia to see me and I was once more reunited with my children. When Patricia got married in August 1978 I had the privilege of giving the bride away.

The years of retirement that stretched before me were to be filled with happiness, busy hobbies and lots of travel. But that is another story.

*1997, author and friend on tour
in front of Saloon "MSM-15"*